Stanley Wells

ROYAL SHAKESPEARE

Four major productions at Stratford-upon-Avon

FURMAN STUDIES

MANCHESTER UNIVERSITY PRESS

FOREWORD

In January 1976, Furman University marked the 150th anniversary of its founding with ceremonies on the campus in Greenville, South Carolina, and the original site of the institution in Edgefield, South Carolina. These occasions provided only the focal points, however, of a series of sesquicentennial events, or "celebrations," throughout the 1975-76 academic session.

Three of these events contributed to liberal learning and knowledge. Alfred Sandlin Reid, Bennette E. Geer Professor of Literature at Furman University, was commissioned to write a history of the University, which was published in April 1976, by the Duke University Press, only a few weeks after Professor Reid's untimely death. The history provides a superb insight into the development of a uniquely American educational phenomenon — the small, church-related liberal arts college. Howard Hanson, one of America's most gifted composers, was commissioned to write a choral composition, which was given its premiere performance at a concert on the Furman campus in May 1976. And Stanley Wells was invited to journey from Stratford-upon-Avon to deliver a series of lectures on plays by William Shakespeare. The lectures were presented in the Recital Hall of the Homozel Mickel Daniel Music Building on the Furman campus on four evenings in late March.

Professor Wells's contributions to Shakespeare studies as critic, editor, theatre historian, and bibliographer are well known to Shakespeare scholars throughout the world. As honorary secretary of the International Shakespeare Conference, sponsored by the Shakespeare Institute, University of Birmingham, and as Director of the Royal Shakespeare Theatre Summer School, he has welcomed hundreds of scholars and students to Stratford-upon-Avon. More particularly, each autumn since November 1969, he and his colleagues of the Shakespeare Institute in Stratford have welcomed groups of Furman students who have concluded a full term of study in England by settling comfortably into residences in Stratford, where they have enjoyed a month of intense study, lectures, and a full season of productions at the Royal Shakespeare Theatre. Professor Wells has become a friend of Furman University; and faculty, students, and alumni were delighted to welcome him to the campus.

The four lectures are a contribution to a growing library of Shakespeare scholarship and criticism which recognizes the significant roles which directors and actors play in increasing our perceptions and our understanding of the remarkable dramas created by a playwright who was also an actor. Professor Wells enjoys a close association with the Royal Shakespeare Theatre, which he serves as a member of the Executive Council of the Board of Governors, and with many directors, actors, and actresses of the Royal Shakespeare Company. He has seen all of the Shakespeare productions at this great theatre since 1958, and the riches of the Theatre archives are easily available to him. In his book *Literature and Drama* (1970) he explores the relationship between reading plays and seeing them performed; in these lectures, while concentrating on the play in a specific performance, he reaches out to a consideration of critical issues and ways in which they can be illuminated by directors and actors.

John H. Crabtree, Jr.

PREFACE

It was an honor and a pleasure for me to be invited to give these lectures at Furman University. I hope it was not felt to be odd that the sesquicentennial of an American university should be commemorated by lectures from an Englishman about English productions of plays by an English writer. Shakespeare's capacity to transcend national boundaries and form a channel for civilized and peaceful communication among the peoples of the world has long been evident. The area of Shakespeare scholarship in which I am working here is one in which America has led the field, with the writings of such distinguished scholars as G.C.D. Odell, Arthur Colby Sprague, and Charles Shattuck, and the collaborative publication projects of the University of Illinois. And one of the ways in which the American bicentennial was celebrated, shortly after I had given my lectures, was a Shakespeare Congress in Washington, at which the Royal Shakespeare Company was represented.

The productions on which I spoke were all ones that I had enjoyed, and this was the main reason for my choice. I also felt that they raised matters of general interest about the plays and their theatrical realization. They illustrate, I think, the general swing from the domination of the actor to the domination of the director. The lectures were illustrated with slides. My gratitude to Dr. John Crabtree for his technical co-operation is only one aspect of a larger debt to him and his family for many kindnesses. I was received with great friendliness and hospitality on Furman's beautiful campus by everyone I met; I should like especially to thank Dr. Francis W. Bonner and Dr. Willard Pate. I am indebted in my work on the lectures to Miss Eileen Robinson and other members of the library staff of the Shakespeare Centre, Stratford-upon-Avon, which houses the archives of the Royal Shakespeare Theatre; to Miss Jeanne Newlin, curator of the Harvard Theatre Collection; to Miss Christine Avern-Carr; and to Mrs. Priscilla Starkey.

Stanley Wells

I

Peter Hall's *Coriolanus*, 1959

Laurence Olivier as Coriolanus and Edith Evans as Volumnia. Photograph by Angus McBean, Harvard Theatre Collection.

In 1959 the Shakespeare Memorial Theatre, like you, had an anniversary to celebrate. It was mounting its one-hundredth season. Celebrations were called for. Stratford likes celebrations. It celebrates Shakespeare's birthday every year; it celebrated his four-hundredth birthday for months on end; it celebrated for two weeks the two-hundredth anniversary of the celebrations that David Garrick organized in 1759; in 1975 it celebrated the centenary of the granting of the charter to the theatre; and undoubtedly in 1979 it will celebrate the centenary of the first season to be performed in that theatre. The celebrations for the hundredth season took place only eighty years after the first season; but they were justified, if justification was needed, by the fact that in some of the intervening years, when seasons sometimes lasted no longer than a week, there had been two of them: one, traditionally, around Shakespeare's birthday, the other in the summer. Glen Byam Shaw had announced in October 1958 that he would retire from his position as Director of the theatre at the end of 1959, and that he would be succeeded by Peter Hall. His final season was to bring an exceptional number of specially distinguished actors to Stratford. Paul Robeson was to play Othello; Dame Edith Evans was to play the Countess in *All's Well That Ends Well,* directed by Tyrone Guthrie; Charles Laughton was to play King Lear, and Bottom in *A Midsummer Night's Dream;* and Sir Laurence Olivier was to play Coriolanus, with Edith Evans as Volumnia, in performances directed by Peter Hall.

Coriolanus was an especially exciting prospect. Dame Edith had not appeared at Stratford since 1913, when, newly recruited to the stage from the millinery business, she had acted Cressida under the direction of William Poel, one of the formative influences on the twentieth century's attitude to the staging of Shakespeare. In the meantime she had become a great name in the history of the English stage, the leading comic actress of her time, famous above all for roles in comedy of manners, in Congreve and in Wilde. Her Lady Bracknell, which she once said she had played in every possible way except under water, was legendary. In Shakespeare she had excelled as Rosalind, as the Nurse in *Romeo and Juliet,* and as Queen Katherine in *Henry VIII.* But her Cleopatra had not been particularly successful; she had yielded the palm in tragic roles to her older contemporary, Dame Sybil Thorndike, who had in fact played Volumnia to Olivier's previous Coriolanus, at the Old Vic in 1938.

Olivier in 1959 was at a high point in his career. He was in his fifty-second year and had behind him a wide range of Shakespearian triumphs, in roles as diverse as Henry V, Justice Shallow, Hotspur, Macbeth, Malvolio, Richard III, and Titus Andronicus. In 1957 he had taken the bold step of appearing at the Royal Court Theatre in the entirely unheroic role of the broken-down comedian, Archie Rice, in John Osborne's *The Entertainer;* and he had been brilliantly successful in this unexpected encounter with the new wave of younger dramatists. He was in fact to be engaged in filming this role during the day while playing Coriolanus in the evenings. Peter Hall, who was to have the responsibility of directing these two great performers in one of Shakespeare's less popular and more difficult plays, was only twenty-eight years old. But he had already directed some distinguished productions, including the first of *Waiting for Godot,* and at Stratford had directed *Love's Labour's Lost* in 1956, *Cymbeline* in 1957, and before *Coriolanus* opened, *A Midsummer Night's Dream* in 1959.

At the time of this production, I was a student at the Shakespeare Institute in Stratford. I had seen Olivier's Richard III in London in 1949, and counted it as my first, most exciting encounter with great acting. I had seen Edith Evans, too, in some of her finest parts, and thought of her with awe. (We were an impressionable lot in those days.) I was excited at the idea of the *Coriolanus* production. I was hoping to be bowled over by it. I have to say this because it may help to explain why indeed I *was* bowled over by it. I saw it the first night, and I saw it again several times — whenever I could spare the time from my thesis and the money from my grant. In talking about it, then, I can call upon personal memories, some of them still very vivid. But memory is fallible. I have also been able to consult documents that are available for public study — the program, the very detailed prompt-book, with ancillary documents, which is in the library of the Shakespeare Centre; a number of photographs; and the reviews. These last, I may say, are less extensive than usual. The first night appears to have coincided with a period of what is now euphemistically called "industrial action," which unfortunately means inaction, in the printing industry. The reviews in newspapers and periodicals are therefore scantier than usual. Easily the best piece that has appeared on the production is an essay by Laurence Kitchin in his *Mid-Century Drama* (1960). It is remarkable that although both *Shakespeare Survey* and *Shakespeare Quarterly* at this period were carrying reviews of Shakespeare productions, neither of them considered this one. The explanation seems to be simply that it opened inconveniently late in the season for their press-dates. It is a measure of the swing towards a theatrically-orientated approach to the study of Shakespeare that we can scarcely imagine a comparable academic neglect of so obviously important a production at the present time.

Coriolanus must have presented both the director and his actors with many problems. It is not one of Shakespeare's most popular plays. The leading role, moreover, is one in which few great actors have succeeded. At least two — Edmund Kean and Henry Irving — failed badly. The most successful was John Philip Kemble; but he had played in a heavily rewritten version, and his merits of statuesque and heavy dignity seem a long way from those of the volatile Laurence Olivier. Of course, Olivier himself had already succeeded in the role; but that was in 1938, when he was only thirty-one years old — a factor of some importance, since so much is made of Coriolanus's physical prowess. The play has appealed especially at times of political turmoil. Kemble first played the role in 1789, the year of the French Revolution. His contemporary, William Hazlitt, wrote about it in political terms, finding that Shakespeare "seems to have had a leaning to the arbitrary side of the question, perhaps from some feeling of contempt for his own origin; and to have spared no occasion of baiting the rabble."[1] In 1934 a version was performed in Paris with the direct intention of provoking revolution and with the actual effect of inciting at least demonstrations and riots in the streets.

Though certainly the play is seriously concerned with political issues, they are continuously bound up with personal ones. Coriolanus's political failure is the result of personal characteristics, and his personality is a preoccupation of many of the play's other characters; taciturn as he is, he might be described as a man more talked about than talking. It is, as Peter Ure says, "an irony of the play that in it most of the characters spend most of their time discussing a hero who cannot bear to be talked about."[2] This interest in character reflects Plutarch's emphasis on the combination in Coriolanus of "many good and evil things together," and it presents the actor of the central role with challenging opportunities.

The play's lack of general appeal has sometimes been attributed partly to its lack of love-story; "but then," as A. C. Bradley points out, "there is none in *Macbeth*, and next to none in *King Lear*."[3] More to the point, perhaps, are the frequent difficulties in Shakespeare's language; his late style makes no concessions, and the verse has little obvious lyricism. The play presents an apparently unremitting seriousness of purpose, an absence of the concern to entertain which is so much to the fore in *Hamlet*, for instance, with its great variety of theatrical appeal. But Olivier is a great comic actor, and he found a surprising amount of comedy in the role of Coriolanus. I shall say more about this later; for the moment it is worth recalling that Bradley, a far-from-frivolous critic, also found comedy in the play:

> When the people appear as individuals they are frequently more or less comical. Shakespeare always enjoyed the inconsequence of the uneducated mind, and its tendency to express a sound meaning in an absurd form. Again, the talk of the servants with one another and with the muffled hero, and the conversation

of the sentinels with Menenius, are amusing. There is a touch of comedy in the contrast between Volumnia and Virgilia when we see them on occasions not too serious. And then, not only at the beginning, as in Plutarch, but throughout the story we meet with that pleasant and wise old gentleman Menenius, whose humour tells him how to keep the peace while he gains his point and to say without offence what the hero cannot say without raising a storm (p. 233).

What Bradley does not remark, however, is the humor that Olivier was able to find in Coriolanus himself.

A final problem worth noting is the play's sheer length. It is one of the five longest of all Shakespeare's plays. In his recent (1975) production of *Hamlet* at the National Theatre, Peter Hall used the full text and spoke out against cutting; but this was not his policy, nor that of the Stratford theatre in general, in 1959. Line counts of the play vary of course, according to the way that prose is spaced out on the page. The promptbook uses Dover Wilson's New Cambridge edition. By my reckoning this has 3325 lines, of which almost 800 were cut, a little less than a quarter of the play. The cuts are fairly distributed among the characters; this is not an example of star roles being emphasized at the expense of lesser ones. Coriolanus loses about 115 lines and Menenius 95. Volumnia loses only about 20, but of course hers is not a long role. It would be easy to disturb the balance of sympathies in this play by selective cutting, but a distinct effort was made to avoid this.

Two scenes were omitted entirely. One is the short scene between a Roman spy and a Volscian soldier (IV.iii). This has been a frequent casualty. It is a pity, especially because the Roman spy's unconcerned treachery forms an effective contrast with Coriolanus's heart-searchings. But the scene does not further the plot, and the fact that it is set in some unidentified locality between Rome and Antium is no doubt an embarrassment when, as here, the production is given on a permanent set. The other scene that was sacrificed is much longer: Act Two, Scene Two, which takes place in the Capitol, and begins with an interesting discussion of Coriolanus by two officers, while they are laying cushions, concluding with the verdict, "He's a worthy man." The scene continues with a formal entrance of the patricians and the tribunes, Menenius's request that Cominius be allowed to speak in favor of Coriolanus's election to the consulship, Coriolanus's refusal to stay while he is praised, Cominius's oration praising Coriolanus's valor, Coriolanus's recall and his request that he be allowed to "o'erleap" the custom of begging for the people's votes, and the tribunes' insistence that he be compelled to do so. It is a strong scene, and its loss must be regretted. The prompt book shows that whereas Act Four, Scene Three was never put into rehearsal, this scene was. Thus it may be assumed that the original intention was to include the scene. The actor most likely to regret its omission is the performer of Cominius, who loses 83 lines of verse. It is fruitless to speculate on the reasons for the omission.

These scenes account for 260 of the 800 omitted lines. The remaining 540 are made up of what are known as internal cuts, that is, of short passages within individual speeches. These include some lines that offer obvious difficulties of vocabulary or syntax to a modern audience, others that amplify what has already been expressed, and some that might be regarded as repetitious. Some of the cuts seem more regrettable than others. I am sorry, for instance, to lose the climax of Aufidius's tribute to Coriolanus at the end of Act Four:

> But he has a merit
> To choke it in the utterance. So our virtues
> Lie in th' interpretation of the time;
> And power, unto itself most commendable,
> Hath not a tomb so evident as a chair
> T'extol what it hath done.

This is a generalizing comment of a kind that is particularly liable to be cut by a director who is concentrating on the play's story line. But it is an interesting remark in relation to the play's insistence on fame and on the relativity of judgment. The virtues of Coriolanus "lie in th' interpretation of the time"; Shakespeare is distancing us, holding us back from judgment, not simply by including this statement, but also by using it as the climax of a tribute to Coriolanus from his greatest enemy. The phrase epitomizes the subtlety of Shakespeare's method. There is something free-standing about his portrayal of Coriolanus which leaves it open to the interpretation of actors and spectators.

On the whole, the cutting seems judicious. Most important, it appears in general to be practical rather than interpretative. The director is not trying to shape our interpretation by manipulating the text. At this time, the Stratford theatre still managed without state subsidy. It is perhaps a measure of the shift from commercial to subsidized theatre that whereas this production had a playing-time of two and a half hours (plus an interval) the following Stratford production of this same play, by John Barton, took three hours (with two intervals), and the most recent, by Trevor Nunn, three hours and ten minutes (with one interval plus a three-minute break).

Peter Hall's handling of the text also included a few minor revisions. In the crowd scenes, for instance, speeches indicated to be spoken by "all" were sometimes allocated to a single actor, no doubt for the sake of clarity.

The revised text gives instructions for laughs and noises from the crowd, who are also given a few additional phrases, such as "Yes, yes!", "To the Capitol!" (I.i.12), and so on.

Coriolanus is not a text that poses serious editorial difficulties, but the promptbook shows that the director gave thought to textual matters. There are one or two apparently considered divergences from Dover Wilson's edition. For instance, in the first scene, according to Dover Wilson, the First Citizen says that what Coriolanus "hath done famously he did it to that end; though soft-conscienced men can be content to say it was for his country, he did it partly to please his mother and to be proud." This, however, is an emendation. The earliest printed text, in the First Folio, reads: "He did it to please his mother and to be partly proud." It is a small enough change, but the reversion to an emphasis on Coriolanus's desire to please his mother acquires significance in the light of the overall interpretation given to the relationship of mother and son. There are one or two other reversions to Folio readings. At a few points, the director has substituted a word still in current use for one used by Shakespeare in a sense that is now obsolete; for example, Coriolanus says: "as high / As I could pitch" — instead of "pick" — "my lance" (I.i, 198), and in the last scene the phrase, "betrayed your business" (l. 92), is altered to "abused our powers." In the promptbook I have noticed only about half-a-dozen examples of this kind of thing.

Although it is only seventeen years since this production was given, there are ways in which it would already seem dated to a modern audience. Theatrical fashions change quickly. The dominant mode in the visual presentation of Shakespeare's plays in the late 1950s was a kind of modified pictorialism deriving from the influence of the Elizabethan revival on the nineteenth-century spectacular tradition. It was a mode that was being eroded under the influence of the Festival Theatre at Stratford, Ontario; but the Stratford-upon-Avon theatre is very much a building of the 1930s. It is structurally incapable of being altered to a thrust-stage theatre, and in 1959 modifications in its basic structure were less extensive than they are now. Plays were commonly presented on a permanent set erected on the stage and having a strong pictorial quality, while nevertheless being capable of modifications during the performance in order to create varied stage pictures appropriate to the changing localities of the scenes.

The setting for *Coriolanus,* designed by Boris Aronson, was a heavy structure placed far forward on the stage. It was not strictly representative of any one place, such as the Forum in Rome, but had steps, gates, and a number of perches and platforms built on a craggy, rock-like structure. A central projection at stage level could be opened to form a kind of inner-stage area. It could also be set with furniture to represent Volumnia's room.

Lighting could focus on this area, but the surrounding structures remained implacably present. Some parts of the structure were movable, however. The gates could be opened, and smoke could issue from them in the scene in which Coriolanus storms the gates of Corioli (I.iv).

The set attracted a good deal of comment, mostly unfavourable. Alfred Alvarez was scornful: it "looked like the first-class saloon of an old transatlantic liner . . . arranged so that all the action was crammed into a few feet at the front of the stage, stifling and airless" *(New Statesman,* 18 July). Kenneth Tynan said it was "mountainous, which is fine, and full of mountainous steps, which is not," and recalled "Alec Guinness' remark, *à propos* of Shakespearean productions in general, that he himself had very few conversations on the stairs of his own house" *(Tynan on Theatre* [Harmondsworth, 1964], p. 94). Laurence Kitchin wrote that it

laid down the rules of the game. This was going to be a vertical production, with coigns of vantage on steps, landings, and an isolated projection resembling the Tarpeian rock. The biggest uninterrupted plane, no bigger than a cramped provincial repertory stage, was bounded by the prompt corner, archaic subtarpeian doors and steps leading up to a city gate. There could be no ceremonial entrances between ranked guards of honour, of the kind Groucho Marx discredited in *Duck Soup* by awaiting his own entrance at the extreme end of a file, neither could a dense mob assemble nor a marching column gather impetus. An immediate effect of the arrangement was that Olivier's first appearance, on top of the rock, did none of the usual things to invite applause. There, like the apparition of an eagle, he suddenly was. (p. 143)

It is possible to offer explanations of some features of the set. In pushing the action forward, as in the fact that no front curtains were used, it was an early move in Peter Hall's efforts to break the barrier of the proscenium arch. The forwardness of the action may also have helped to overcome acoustic problems — the theatre is not easy in this respect — and the smallness of the playing area may have helped to disguise the fact that the crowds were rather small.

Coriolanus is not one of Shakespeare's more musical plays. There are no songs, and most of the original music cues are for martial instruments: for drums, trumpets, and cornets. In keeping with a fashion of the time, this production used *musique concrète,* a combination of music and sound effects prerecorded and played on a tape during the performance. A distinguished composer, Roberto Gerhard, was responsible for this, and he achieved striking, sometimes indeed shattering, effects with unconventional instruments such as gongs and tam-tams.

The music was one way in which the director dealt with one of the play's theatrical problems, its unusual form. In most of Shakespeare's plays about warfare the battle scenes come at the end, as a climax. Even in *Macbeth,* in which, as in *Coriolanus,* the hero's valor is important, the action begins at the end of a battle, not in the thick of it. But in *Coriolanus* the battle scenes come early in the play. There is a danger that the director and his actors will exhaust their energies in the early scenes, and that the rest of the play will be a long anti-climax. Peter Hall certainly did not try to minimize the potential excitement of these scenes. At the opening, the lights dimmed on the uncurtained set, to be followed by a racket of bells, shouts, crowd-noises, and beating sounds working up to a climax as the mob broke through the gates on to the stage. It was a "thrilling opening" (A. Pryce-Jones, *Observer,* 12 July), causing Frank Granville-Barker to write: "From the moment . . . that the Roman mob surged on to the stage — vomited, as it seemed, from the very bowels of the earth — my attention was gripped." Sound effects were used in the scenes that followed to reinforce the noise made by the comparatively small stage armies. But Peter Hall also used musical and lighting effects as a means of articulating the scenes and effecting transitions of mood. He was careful to create a theatrical structure which would relax as well as create tension, so that the audience would not be excessively stretched. In the first act there was an episode of domestic repose in the scene with Volumnia and her ladies, introduced by soothing music. The battle scenes that followed were un-doubtedly noisy, but there was some effectively peaceful and eerie music for the return to Rome at the beginning of the second act. The scenes of Coriolanus's begging for the people's voices were a relaxed interlude before the mounting climax of his banishment, and the first movement of the play as performed came at the end of Act Four, Scene Two, in which Volumnia berates the tribunes. It was a powerful and emotional scene. Volumnia's strong exit was usually greeted with applause, leaving Menenius to give the first part a quiet ending with his words "Fie! fie! fie!" spoken slowly and thoughtfully as he made a slow exit.

This placing of the single interval means that it was followed by several comparatively relaxed scenes. The beginning of Act Four, Scene Six was calculated as an idyllic glimpse of Rome at peace. As the critic of *The Scotsman* (14 July) put it, "We are given a glimpse of the happiness which follows his banishment, when the mob leader passes over the stage carrying his youngest child on his shoulders, and followed by the rest of his family, as if he were bound for a day at the seaside." It was a calculated point of repose, with Sicinius and Brutus, the uncles of the people, compla-cently and patronizingly benevolent, as if the achievement were theirs. But the peace was soon disturbed by the breathless entrances of messengers with news of the advance of the Volscian armies, disturbing and angering the tribunes; and emotional tension was high through the fluctuating rhythms of the remaining episodes. The theatrical rhythm of a play is different in each production, according to the cuts in the text, the moments chosen by the actors for their climaxes, and many other factors. Peter Hall, helped by his musicians and actors, seemed to me to create a satisfying shape for this production.

I have been speaking so far mainly about matters which are the province and responsibility of the director rather than the actors. But I have laid stress on the importance in this play of individual personality within the no-less-important political framework, and no doubt this was in the director's mind when he cast his performers. The company included many actors of impressive physical appearance, manly in voice and move-ment, and this enabled some of the less important roles to be appropriately and strongly cast. The company included, too, some talented younger performers, who have since risen to greater prominence and were already showing their abilities. For example, Roy Dotrice and Ian Holm, both of them now star actors, played two of the servants in Aufidius's house. These are brilliantly written cameo parts, in which Shakespeare uses individualizing comic touches both to create entertainment and to show a kinship between the Volscian commoners and the Roman ones. Like the individual members of the Roman mob, these serving men are easily swayed; their engaging mutability is the reverse of Coriolanus's stern integrity and is fittingly juxtaposed with it. Holm and Dotrice were not among the more heroically-built members of the company, and this fact assisted the comedy of their feeble efforts to resist Coriolanus, and the bravado of their protestations in his absence. They were not altogether helped by the Welsh accents which they were required to adopt as a device for distinguishing the Volscians from the Romans; but they realized the potential within their roles with a sharp, well-timed immediacy that was capable of raising loud laughter.

On the opposing side, the Roman citizens were led by another actor who has since risen to greater heights, Albert Finney, now playing Hamlet for Peter Hall at the National Theatre. Then only twenty-three years old, he had already played Macbeth at the Birmingham Repertory Theatre. He was Olivier's understudy as Coriolanus and played the role several times. A big, brawny, barrel-chested man, he played the First Citizen with a natural authority combined with a mutinously hang-dog look, a man with a chip on his shoulder who attracted sympathy all the same. Like other actors of his generation, he retained a local accent even when playing classical parts, and the Roman citizens had Lancashire accents to oppose to the Welsh of the Volscians. The lesser women's parts were played by Mary Ure, as Virgilia, and by Vanessa Redgrave, aged twenty-two, as Valeria.

There was strong casting, too, in the middle-range parts. Robert Hardy, later to play Coriolanus himself for BBC television, was one of the tribunes; the other was Peter Woodthorpe. Several times the action narrows to a focus on this sinister pair, and I have never been so conscious of their Rosencrantz-and-Guildenstern-like affinity. Paul Hardwick was a bluff, manly Cominius, strong of voice and physique but easily touched, and with a soldierly tenderness towards Coriolanus. In the other camp, Anthony Nicholls, no less convincing as a warrior, was suaver in speech and manner, a political realist whose admiration for Coriolanus went unquestioned, but whose treachery came as no surprise. As an upper-class Volscian, he was not required to adopt a Welsh accent — obviously he had been sent to public school over the border — but he and his officers wore furs that were occasionally more suggestive of Danny La Rue than of the barbarism they were doubtless meant to evoke.

The Menenius was Harry Andrews, who played many principal supporting roles in Stratford productions. He too is a big man, and his natural authority was helpful in his dealings with the citizens. Menenius is an ambiguous figure. When John Barton directed the play in 1967, he pointed out in a program note that Menenius is usually played as "a centre of sympathy, a choric figure," but suggested that we should see him rather as a "political old-hand . . . motivated more by his sense of his own skill as a manipulator than by love for his country and friends." Whichever view we take, this draws attention to a point of central interest in the play; that is, the extent to which a man may adapt himself to a situation without compromising his own integrity. Coriolanus finds this intensely difficult. The Roman spy has no problems at all. The most obvious manipulators in the play are the tribunes, who play upon the sympathies and weaknesses of the citizens like a pair of unscrupulous shop-stewards. Menenius, too, knows how to handle the citizens, and commands their sympathetic interest with his fable of the belly. But he also speaks deprecatingly, even contemptuously, of them: "Rome and her rats are at the point of battle . . . though abundantly they lack discretion, / Yet are they passing cowardly."

How are we to take this? Is he just a smooth operator, or rather (as Bradley suggests) a wise, just, and statesmanlike figure? Harry Andrews certainly leaned to the latter interpretation, playing the character very much from his own point of view, as a sincere statesman, devoted to the cause of the patricians, and personally devoted to Coriolanus, but genuinely concerned, nevertheless, for the citizens, and regretful at their folly. He was impressive in his anxious but controlled attempts to conciliate the tribunes in their rabble-rousing incitements of the crowd against Coriolanus, as also, a scene or two later, when he has to apply similar palliatives to Coriolanus's wrath against the tribunes. Harry Andrews can convey an impression of inner strength and calm which contrasted with Coriolanus's lack of self-control. He did indeed seem like a wise centre in the play, emphasized by his presence alone on-stage just before the interval. His words, "Fie! fie! fie!" might go for very little, but he sighed them out, well separated one from another, shaking his head as he moved off, in a way that certainly suggested the sagacious observer, saddened by experience. He was moving, too, in his reactions to Coriolanus's later rejection of his pleading.

We are lucky enough to have some inside information about how one of the leading performers approached her role. Dame Edith Evans spoke to the annual Theatre Summer School on 21 August. Her talk was called, a little coyly and also a little defensively, "A Little Talk," and was concerned with her role of Volumnia. I was present, and I remember feeling the star quality of a great actress in these circumstances as strongly as in her stage performances. The hall was crowded. Before she began to speak she removed a wrap from her shoulders and hung it on the back of a chair, giving the audience a sly glance which, for no easily discernible reason, suddenly had us all eating out of her hand. The talk was reported in both *The Times* (22 August) and the *Times Educational Supplement* (28 August). Like many actors speaking in public, she was anxious not to seem to be giving a lecture; and, also like many actors speaking in public, she beat most lecturers at their own game. *The Times* reported her as saying that when she "accepted the part she had neither seen nor read the play — oh yes, that often happens with me, we were assured. She had, however, a preconceived notion. Volumnia surely was a bloodthirsty old harridan. 'How' — with a glance at Mr. Glen Byam Shaw in her audience — 'how could I possibly be a bloodthirsty old harridan?' Mr. Byam Shaw . . . had asked her to remember that Volumnia lived somewhere about the fourth century B.C. That was something. There was no need to excuse Volumnia for not having heard about turning the other cheek. She was a pagan, a Roman, and a patrician." The *Times Educational Supplement* varies the report: "There was none of that 'loving your enemies' nonsense: you had enemies, and you hated them." She "said that she knew about Rome: she had been there three times recently and seen all the columns."

Still, she had to discover the woman in Volumnia, and to play her as a woman. "After all, at her first appearance Volumnia brings her sewing, and she and the women sit at stools — 'That's a friendly little opening, isn't it?' In his first scene she talks about Coriolanus' honour, and it is very strong meat. It's all very strong stuff — but they're *sewing!*''

She found Volumnia's womanliness in her love for her son, whom she
described as "a very arrogant boy. He displeases — what do you call it? —
the Labour Party. She pleads with him not to antagonize them: he should get
power first and afterwards he can antagonize them as much as he likes.''
(T.E.S.) She spoke about how an actress has to find in the words that she
speaks a reality that is meaningful to herself. "When she meets her son after
his triumph she is almost too excited to be coherent. 'What is it — Coriolanus
must I call thee?' In other words 'What's this thing they have pinned on you,
darling? The V.C.?' She went on to stress the personal rather than the
political in Volumnia. His banishment is not only a crying injustice done to
him but also means that he will be completely cut off from her. That is what
provokes her to anger, Juno-like, 'and of course,' adds Edith Evans, 'one has
to do the best one can with *that!*' ''

Dame Edith was interesting on Volumnia's physical appearance when
she goes to appeal to Coriolanus on behalf of Rome, and on her return to
Rome. "When she sees him again her raiment and state of body ought indeed
to show what her life has been since Coriolanus' exile. In the eighteenth
century a tragedy queen would dress like a tragedy queen for this scene.
Quite wrong, thinks Edith Evans, Volumnia has in fact been wasting away.
And at the end, when she has won him over, doesn't she realize that, instead
of getting him back, she has lost him a second time, almost certainly for
good? He will go back to Corioli to face the music, and she will go back to
Rome. No wonder she has nothing to say to the Romans when they welcome
her'' *(The Times)*.

Dame Edith's talk was amusing, and was reported with appreciation of
this. We were reminded as we listened that it was given by the greatest living
exponent of Restoration comedy. But it also made some brilliantly revealing
points about both the play and the way in which a modern actress may
approach a classical part. Dame Edith was not type-cast as Volumnia. Her
strength had been mainly in comic and melodramatic roles. Her style is
unquestionably mannered, though it has to be said that in this very season
she had played the Countess of Rousillon in *All's Well That Ends Well,* with
a tranquil, elegiac beauty, as well as a queenly dignity, that was profoundly
moving. Though she has a fine presence, she is not heavily dominating. In its
report of her talk, *The Times* said that she "was speaking in the Conference
Hall [that is, the rehearsal room behind the main theatre] where she had
begun rehearsing the part. There the producer, Mr. Peter Hall, had asked her
to do just one thing: to add two feet to her stature. For that she had had to
wait till they moved into the theatre itself . . .'' The effort, it must be
admitted, was occasionally visible. Dame Edith was a little over 70 years old

She was in very good physical shape, but, as she implied in her talk, she was not too obviously qualified to represent a "bloodthirsty old harridan." The effort sometimes showed. She had a habit of nervously clenching and unclenching her fists that could be distracting. The mannerisms in her wonderful voice, her capacity to color a phrase, to suggest infinite nuances of expression, were not obviously suited to the more strident aspects of Volumnia's character. It seemed a bit like asking a born Susanna to sing Brunhilde. But the training and experience of a great actress were evident both in the way she found those aspects of the role that most suited her, and, more courageously, faced the need to act against her natural stage presence. She demonstrated the classical actress's skill in responding to the role's varied vocal demands, ranging from the chatty domesticity of the opening scene — in which she is sewing — to the fierce anger of her denunciation of the tribunes and the incantatory grandeur called for by

> Before him he carries noise, [and] behind him he leaves tears:
> Death, that dark spirit, in's nervy arm doth lie,
> Which, being advanced, declines, and then men die. (II.i. 156-9)

In the later scenes the colorful extravagance of her first gown was replaced by mourning black, for the reasons explained in her talk; grief predominated to the extent that some critics found monotony in her speaking of the long plea to Coriolanus. Her return to Rome was that of a woman who knew she had failed, though she was greeted with triumph. Kenneth Tynan complained that her "fussy, warbling vibrato swamps all too often the meaning of the lines," and the critic of the *Glasgow Herald* found that "Her voice instead of sounding forceful and resonant, was more often querulous." These were first-night reactions. I saw the performance several times, and felt that although Dame Edith was not always at her best, when she was, such criticisms seemed quite irrelevant. Even on the first night, *The Times* found that her "rating of the Tribunes is quite unforgettable." In this scene, she could suggest the womanly aspects of Volumnia simultaneously with the tyrannical ones. At its strongest, her voice here was indeed "forceful and resonant." The scene ends with the lines about her being provoked "to anger, Juno-like," of which she said in her talk "one has to do the best one can with *that!*" Her best was magnificent: profoundly strong, but never inhuman.

The production is, of course, remembered mainly for its central performance, Olivier's Coriolanus. Before talking about it, I should like to say something about his style and reputation as an actor. He was, at this time, acknowledged, along with Sir John Gielgud, as the head of his profession. Any performance by him in a major classical role was sure to arouse excitement. He also is an intensely individual and idiosyncratic actor who can create violent reactions of antipathy as well as admiration. He is famous for his athleticism and for technical self-consciousness. He looks different in every role he plays and will go to endless trouble to perfect an accent or to create appropriate make-up. He is, in short, a virtuoso; and virtuosity can create antipathy. Some members of an audience will be carried away by it; others will remain aloof, aware of technical brilliance but also somewhat repelled by it. I give way to it all the time; but the minority of critics who responded adversely to Olivier's performance seem to have been reacting against his virtuosity. Alan Brien, for instance, wrote: "I would ask for less consciousness on Olivier's part that every word is putty and can be moulded to his whim. I would ask for less technique — instead I would like to feel that the lines are mastering him occasionally . . . I would ask for less decoration, less bravura, less personality, less expertise" (*Spectator,* 17 July). To me that seems ungrateful; but I can, by an effort of the imagination, understand something of the objection.

Laurence Kitchin's excellent essay on Olivier's performance is virtually a defence of it against Alan Brien's kind of accusation. Kitchin praises Olivier's "interpretative intelligence of a very high order" which, he says, had been brought "to bear on this role; he was not intelligent only in action, from point to point." Kitchin's essay is so good a piece of interpretation that I cannot compete with it; but I will try to describe some of the salient features of Olivier's performance.

His make-up seemed designed to hide some of the quick intelligence of his face. He wore a black wig and was beetle-browed, heavier looking than usual. The bridge of his nose was built up, his mouth arrogantly snarled, his knit eyebrows scornfully lifted. His walk and stance emphasized the warrior. As he addressed the mob he clenched his fists, bunched his muscles, and inflated his chest, looking, as Kitchin puts it, like "some ruggedly aggressive Roman statue." He is a master of gesture that is both characterful and graceful; there was a strange beauty in the way he wielded his sword, or disposed his arms and hands as he invited his men to follow him through the gates of Corioli. Here he seemed in his element. Here we saw the positive side, the value, of his arrogance. In the battle scenes no less than in the scenes in Rome, Coriolanus is contemptuous of the men to whom he owes part of his success. But Olivier showed us that the scorn which he pours on his men is inseparable from the anger and energy which impel him in his fights against the common enemy, and which inspire his followers to do all they can to support him. The example of inspiring courage — even foolhardiness — which he gave in the battles of the opening act was powerful enough to make us believe that, like many warriors after him, he could be hero-worshipped by his men in action, even though they might later lose confidence in him as a peace-time leader.

One of the attributes of a great actor is, I suppose, the capacity to suggest complexity of character. It is also, of course, one of the attributes of a great playwright. Both can make us feel contact with the richness of human experience, with the surprising inconsistencies in human behavior, the unexpected thoughts or actions which, when they are revealed, seem much truer than the expected. The audience's reaction to these can be one of delighted laughter, as it so often is with Falstaff, Shakespeare's greatest creation of this kind. Olivier's Coriolanus, too, often provoked this sort of laughter. I have said that he is a great comic actor, and his discovery of potential comedy in the role was one of his ways of accommodating it to his own genius, just as Dame Edith had found Volumnia's womanliness. He found comedy in his coy, bashful, perhaps vain rejection of praise for his prowess in battle, and in his affectionate hyperbole about his mother's strength of character. He roused a big laugh with

> Nay, mother,
> Resume that spirit when you were wont to say
> If you had been the wife of Hercules,
> Six of his labours you'ld have done, and saved
> Your husband so much sweat.

But the scene in which this quality was most apparent was that in which Coriolanus is shown in external conflict with his mother, Menenius, and Cominius, and in internal conflict with himself, about whether he can apologize to the people in order to improve his standing with them. The obvious way to play the scene (III.ii) would, I suppose, be with a depressed earnestness, Coriolanus grimly, even despairingly, forcing himself to behave against his nature. Olivier gave it instead with a lightness of touch which amused but was, perhaps, no less essentially serious. The sense of a man trying but failing to resist domination by his mother was strong here, and was increased by Volumnia's addition of "my son" in the line "Prithee now, [my son,] say you will, and go about it" (l. 98) and by the anger in her parting words: "Do your will" — as it were, "Do what the hell you like, I wash my hands of you." Kitchin describes how Olivier "listened to his mother's reproofs with infantile sullenness . . . An habitual battle of wills, fought out not so long ago about apologizing for rough words or the breaking of a companion's toy, was being reopened." There is one particularly fine speech in which Coriolanus torments himself with a vision of the prostitution he must undergo which becomes so vivid that he rejects it with the words, "I will not do it." They might be spoken violently, but Olivier paused and spoke the words quietly as if with sudden acknowledgment of the truth within himself, and burst into anger against a further attempt to persuade him before the audience's delayed laughter showed that it had taken the point.

In Volumnia's ensuing rebuke of his pride, Olivier listened with a mocking appearance of deference which revealed his true feeling. Then his plea that he would do as he was told had the comic quality of a little boy seeking approval though he knows he has been naughty. At the end of the scene Menenius and Cominius are still trying to keep him in order. He will speak to the people. "Ay, but mildly," says Menenius. "Well, mildly be it then — mildly," replies Coriolanus. But instead of speaking the final word, Olivier, after a long pause, simply mouthed it, achieving, as Kitchin says, an "unforgettable effect."

Not everyone capitulated to Olivier's comic treatment of this scene; and it has to be admitted that it was accompanied by a certain amount of mouthing and tongue-rolling that perhaps too strongly recalled the music-hall vulgarities of Archie Rice. But an actor's treatment of individual scenes has to be considered in the context of the performance as a whole. In the scene following this one, Coriolanus has to deliver some of his most forceful denunciations of the people, culminating in the speech beginning, "You common cry of curs . . ." If we had already had anger in the scene with his mother, the effect might have become monotonous. The light handling of the earlier scene made for greater contrasts, and left Olivier with amazing energy for the full explosion of his pent-up rage, triggered by Sicinius's accusation, "You are a traitor to the people."

The air was highly charged for the rest of the scene, but for his final speech Coriolanus had regained a degree of self-control and spoke with comparative calm. Kitchin had seen Olivier's earlier performance in the role and wrote:

> Two decades had scarcely dimmed my memory of his 'You common cry of curs!' . . . Now the delivery was changed. Just before this speech Olivier leaned against the masonry high up on Aronson's set, head rolling from side to side, eyes mad as those of a Sistine Chapel prophetess while he listened to the tribunes. The head movement, I was amused to notice, was one recommended by Elsie Fogerty to her students for relaxing tension in the neck; Olivier was preparing himself. Advancing to the Tarpeian projection on which we had first seen him, he made the speech with less volume than in Casson's production, but with a terrifying concentration of contempt. People who think him a prose actor, because he so often breaks up lines, overlook his sustained power in a passage of invective like this . . . he gave the phrases such a charge of emotion that he gathered them into a single rhetorical missile, so that the speech had an impact like jagged stones parcelled together and hurled in somebody's face.

Edith Evans had found that much of Volumnia's motive force derived from adoration of her son. Olivier's Coriolanus derived much of its power from tension between two strong relationships: the domination of his mother, from which he could never quite escape; and his paradoxical admiration for Aufidius, his greatest enemy. The speeches before Antium were gently, quietly given. The awe he inspired in Aufidius's servants, before they knew who he was, helped him, appropriately to the text, to regain a sense of identity in the "world elsewhere"; and with Aufidius his personality found a temporary release and wholeness that it could never command in Rome. Laurence Kitchin found that "There was no doubt at all where the play's climax comes. It is on the sealing of their pact, or so I shall always believe after Olivier's extraordinary handshake." But a man is not "author of himself." Coriolanus successfully turns Menenius away, and the episode was movingly performed. But from his mother's entry, his fall was seen to be inevitable, and his capitulation to Volumnia, as he held "her by the hand, silent," was as moving as it should be.

Olivier kept his most startling effect of all for the moment of his death. Indeed, it is said that not even his fellow-actors knew how he would perform this scene until a very late stage in the proceedings; and this is borne out by the fact that the pencilled directions in the prompt-book overlay others that have been erased. Kenneth Tynan's description cannot be bettered:

> At the close, faithful as ever to the characterization on which he has fixed, Olivier is roused to suicidal frenzy by Aufidius' gibe — 'thou boy of tears!' '*Boy!*' shrieks the overmothered general, in an outburst of strangled fury, and leaps up a flight of precipitous steps to vent his rage. Arrived at the top, he relents and throws his sword away. After letting his voice fly high in the great, swingeing line about how he 'flutter'd your Volscians in *Cor-i-ol-i*', he allows a dozen spears to impale him. He is poised, now, on a promontory some twelve feet above the stage, from which he topples forward, to be caught by the ankles so that he dangles, inverted, like the slaughtered Mussolini. A more shocking, less sentimental death I have not seen in the theatre; it is at once proud and ignominious, as befits the titanic fool who dies it.

Olivier created a startling visual image of Coriolanus's downfall, the more ironically effective in that the rostrum on which he was stabbed was that from which he had berated the mob on his first entry, and from which he had cursed the "common cry of curs." When he fell from it with a strangulated cry, to be caught by the ankles and held dangling while Aufidius stabbed him in the belly, the magnitude and the squalor of his fall were epitomized. Philip Hope-Wallace found it "overwhelmingly tragic" (*Manchester Guardian,* 9 July), but it had its critics. Glynne Wickham is clearly girding at it when, in an essay on performances of the play, he writes: "it is

22

easy to obliterate the tragic stature of Coriolanus in a matter of seconds by allowing him to leap to his death in the manner of a trapeze-artist for the sake of the gasp of surprise in the auditorium.''[4] But that is ungenerous. The fall was a final, climactic assertion of Coriolanus's grandeur in the moment of his death, the last of a series of strokes with which Olivier had portrayed the bewildering many-sidedness of the character. It was theatrical; but we were in a theatre. It was dangerous; but Coriolanus lived, as well as died, dangerously. It was the final shock for an audience that had been given many surprises, and it left me, at least, overcome with awe. I left the theatre, on the first night, profoundly impressed, and walked the streets of Stratford for twenty minutes before feeling I wanted to talk to anyone. That, I think, is what Aristotle meant by catharsis.

FOOTNOTES

1. *The Characters of Shakespeare's Plays, 1817* (London, World's Classics, 1916, etc.), p. 56.
2. *Elizabethan and Jacobean Drama,* edited by J.C. Maxwell (Liverpool, 1974), p. 17.
3. *"Coriolanus"* (1912), reprinted in *Studies in Shakespeare,* edited by Peter Alexander (London, 1964), pp. 219-237.
4. *"Coriolanus:* Shakespeare's Tragedy in Rehearsal and Performance,'' *Later Shakespeare,* Stratford-upon-Avon Studies 8, edited by Bernard Harris and John Russell Brown (London, 1966), pp. 167-181; p. 169.

II

Peter Hall's *Hamlet*, 1965

David Warner as Hamlet. Photograph by Thomas F. Holte.

In May 1965, a little over three months before his production of *Hamlet* was due to open at what was by then the Royal Shakespeare Theatre, Peter Hall lectured on the subject of *"Hamlet* Today" at the Shakespeare Institute. That lecture formed the basis for a talk which he gave to his company of actors when rehearsals started, and a condensed version of which was printed in the theatre program. He spoke of the play's susceptibility to varied interpretations, describing it as "one of mankind's great images," which "turns a new face to each century, even to each decade. It is a mirror which gives back the reflection of the age that is contemplating it." He showed an awareness, that is, of the danger that the play will be interpreted in terms of the interpreter, that interpretation is "a minimizing process . . . difficult to avoid" (*Times*, 10 May), that "any interpretation must limit" (program) and that, though "the director's duty was to interpret it for his own time . . . he was in peril of over-stressing certain elements at the expense of others."

In these remarks Mr. Hall stressed both the desirability and the difficulty of taking an objective view of the play, of responding to it in its own terms instead of reshaping it to our own preconceptions and predilections. He was glancing at a kind of historical approach which would not be pedantic, but would enable the play to strike us with a fresh and true impact, instead of being moulded cosily to our own ways of thought. From this, one might have expected him to go on to advocate a retreat from interpretation, a degree of neutrality in theatrical presentation which would aim at allowing the play to speak in its own terms. But Mr. Hall did not heed his own warning to the extent of denying himself the liberty of interpretation. Indeed, he said later: "You should approach a classic with the maximum of scholarship you can muster — and then you honestly try to interpret what you think it means to a person living now."[1] In his lecture he approached his interpretation by talking of the play's central character, and then followed the method that Hazlitt attributed to Hamlet himself, of transferring "the distresses of Hamlet . . . to the general account of humanity."[2]

Hamlet, said Peter Hall, "is trembling on the point of full maturity. He is about to jell. He may go either way. He has within him the possibility of all virtues or all vices, but at this crucial point in his development he is tried by an extreme crisis. His love for his mother, and for his father, his attitude towards sex, his feeling for his friends, for his country, his political responsibilities, his honour, his philosophy, his religion, whether he is man or animal, king or commoner — all these are suddenly torn apart. He is crucified by an experience so complex that it leads to a profound disillusionment and finally to a terrible fatalism." Mr. Hall went on to link this diagnosis of Hamlet's spiritual condition with an interpretation of the social and intellectual situation in the decade to which the face of *Hamlet* was then turned. "For our decade I think the play will be about the disillusionment which produces an apathy of the will so deep that commitment to politics, to religion or to life is impossible." Hamlet suffered from a "disease of disillusionment" which stopped "the final, committed action." And this emotion existed in young people at the time: "To me it is extraordinary that in the last 15 years the young of the West, and particularly the intellectuals, have by and large lost the ordinary, predictable radical impulses which the young in all generations have had. You might march against the Bomb. But on the other hand, you might not. You might sleep with everyone you know, or you might not. You might take drugs, you might not. There is a sense of what-the-hell-anyway, over us looms the Mushroom Cloud . . . This negative response is deep and appalling."

By the time Peter Hall directed *Hamlet* he had been overall director of the Stratford theatre for five years, during which he had greatly expanded its activities and its budget. He had had a major success the previous year with his collaborative production of a cycle of Shakespeare's English history plays, known as *The Wars of the Roses,* and David Addenbrooke has written that his "fascination with politics and political structures was further expounded in his 1965 production of *Hamlet,* which was in many ways, a natural growth out of the pre-occupations of *The Wars of the Roses"* (p. 129). The history plays had been considerably rewritten by the co-producer, John Barton, with an added emphasis on their political aspects, so that they represented a very direct attempt to project an interpretation not only of Shakespeare but also of history. The directors were, in a sense, writing their own plays alongside Shakespeare's.

Hamlet was not treated so radically. It was not rewritten in the way that transformed *The Wars of the Roses.* Nevertheless this was a very positive interpretation of the play which affords an interesting opportunity to consider the methods of the interpretative director. How is it that a director can, as it were, project his opinions about a play at the same time as presenting the play itself? Does the play not have its own voice? How much of the meaning of a play is determined by the author, how much by his interpreters? There are no simple answers to these questions, but a consideration of some aspects of Peter Hall's production of *Hamlet* may enable us to see some of the ways in which the interpreter can speak through his performance. This will be my theme in the first part of my talk today; from that, I shall hope to go on to speak about the way in which modern intellectual attitudes may affect interpretations of the play.

I have said that the script of this production was not rewritten, but it was considerably shortened. The text of *Hamlet* offers many problems. It is fluid, in the sense that it appeared in varying forms in Shakespeare's time and that we have no definitive version; and it is very long. Just occasionally, the play is performed in a complete text, which means a conflation of the "good" quarto and the Folio. It is interesting that Peter Hall does this in his current production, at the National Theatre. In 1965, however, he omitted about 730 lines — that is to say, about one-fifth of the whole play.[3] This means that he was using a longer text than most.[4] The cuts were of the kind known as internal; that is, no whole scenes were omitted, nor were any characters. This avoided such "traditional" omissions as the Polonius/Reynaldo scene, and the characters of Cornelius and Voltimand.

It is not always easy to speculate on the reasons for textual omissions. Many of those made in this version could be attributed to causes other than the desire to slant the interpretation in particular ways. They include passages offering textual or linguistic problems (*e.g.* I.iv. 36-38, the "dram of eele"); passages which create difficulty for the actor, such as Laertes's failure to restrain his tears at Ophelia's death (IV. vii. 186-9); topical passages, such as the satire on the boys' acting companies in Act Two, Scene Two; the Gravedigger's satire on courtiers and lawyers; and amplificatory passages, where the point may be considered already to have been satisfactorily made, as in the extended satire of Osric. Indeed, when one looks at acting-texts of Shakespeare, one is occasionally tempted to sympathize with Dr. Johnson's criticism that he sometimes affects "a wearisome train of circumlocution."[5]

Directors are particularly prone to excising passages descriptive of staged action. Thus Peter Hall omitted, for example, two of Horatio's descriptions of the Ghost, which the audience has already seen (I.ii. 202-206, 215-219). More regrettably, though understandably in a play as long as *Hamlet,* passages in which the characters indulge in reflective comment on their situation, or generalize from it, are likely to suffer; thus the conversation between Hamlet, Rosencrantz, and Guildenstern about dreams (II.ii. 261-274) was sacrificed, as were Rosencrantz's lines beginning, "The cess of majesty" (III.iii. 15-22). The play-within-the-play is usually felt to be more important for its effect on the king than for what the characters say, and their speeches are frequently shortened; in this production they lost thirty-six lines, mostly of a generalizing tendency. Directors are also inclined to omit passages written in styles remote from the basic norm; so in this production certain rhetorical or grandiloquent passages were omitted, such as Laertes's

> tears seven times salt
> Burn out the sense and virtue of mine eye! . . .

Cuts like these have a "flattening" effect on the play's language. They make things easier for the actor, but reduce the play's range of style. Some missions may be attributed to a desire to offer a particular view of a haracter. Polonius, for example, loses many amplificatory passages that ctors often use to make a comic point, and though these cuts may be ttributed to the desire to shorten the play, they also fit in with the decision of he director and his actor to present Polonius as shrewder and more cunning han he has usually been played.

The reviewer for *The Times* complained that Horatio "almost vanishes o as to preserve Hamlet's isolation," but this is not strongly supported by he text. Admittedly, he lost his expression of concern for Hamlet's safety in is encounter with the Ghost (I.iv. 68-79), and the complexity of the charac- er was reduced by the omission of his rather puzzling statement that Hamlet vas not responsible for the deaths of Rosencrantz and Guildenstern. His part vas cut by about seventy-five lines, but he was always on-stage when he hould have been. The reviewer's impression may have been due partly to he fact that the character was not very positively played, and that the elationship between Hamlet and Horatio was not stressed. Perhaps the irector regretted this. In his new production, Horatio is strongly played as a nan considerably older than Hamlet, and many reviewers commented avorably on the performance.

There may be interpretative significance in the fact that Hamlet was leprived of his assertion of his duty to kill Claudius:

> And is't not to be damned
> To let this canker of our nature come
> In further evil?   (V.ii. 68-70)

his omission fits in with the director's view of Hamlet as incapable of "the inal, committed action." The interpretation of Claudius, too, may have een assisted by cuts; the Ghost's contrast of himself and Claudius was educed (by I.v. 48-52), which conformed with the suave exterior of this Claudius; and his appearance of political efficiency was increased by the mission of a qualification at II. ii. 81-3.

Although the omissions in Peter Hall's text have interpretative conse- uences, he should not be accused of serious textual manipulation in the nterests of presenting his personal view of the play. The setting and cos- umes, designed by John Bury, certainly helped him. The set was permanent n some respects, but it could be rapidly rearranged. Beyond a black false- roscenium arch, from behind which entrances could be made, two great lack walls slanted inwards, their further ends separated by two massive oors. In each wall were two tall panels, which could be removed to reveal ookshelves for Polonius's study; grandiose, fleshy frescoes for certain ourt scenes; which could create large apertures for the open-air scene

showing Fortinbras with his army (IV. iv.); and on one of which a wa
monument could be fixed for the graveyard scene. The doors at the bac
could open to reveal more frescoes, a view of the sky for the Fortinbra
scene, a broken funeral column for the graveyard scene, or neutral wall
which extended the playing area. The stage floor was part of the setting
geometrically patterned in black and white. Shiny and marmoreally solid, i
was fine for the palace scenes, but meant that the digging of Ophelia's grav
resembled a major archaeological exercise, and that we had to try to ignor
it in the Fortinbras scene. Costumes were of no clearly defined period
They had affinities with Tudor dress, but "the entire court were robed in
pin-striped material, to suggest a world of officialdom" (Addenbrooke, p
130).

Stage properties also played their part in the interpretative effect of th
settings. As we entered the theatre, we were confronted by the mouth of
great cannon in the middle of the uncurtained stage: an initial martia
image. In the first court scene, the king and his party were wheeled forwar
on a low, movable platform, creating, I suppose, a sense of mechanize
efficiency which was not without its ludicrous aspect. Hamlet was seate
unhappily between the king and Polonius, looking acutely embarrassed
Hamlet's interview with his mother should properly take place in a close
but, as has become customary in modern productions, Peter Hall set it in
bedroom; curtains cut off the back part of the stage, and an immense doubl
bed was centrally placed. Fortinbras's army was accompanied by a can
non, a cart, and a siege engine.

The stage directions in Shakespeare's plays often call for unspecifie
numbers of anonymous lords, servants, soldiers, and so on, who ca
contribute in various ways to the interpretation. At the beginning of Ac
One, Scene Two of *Hamlet,* for example, the quarto direction opens wit
the word "flourish," and calls for some "counsellors"; the list of speakin
characters ends with the phrase "cum aliis" ("with others"), who mus
include Voltimand and Cornelius. An economical director could get awa
with a single, off-stage trumpet-call and a couple of attendant lords. Bu
Peter Hall took the opportunity, equally offered him by the stage direction
of presenting an elaborate display of courtly ritual. The court party wa
guarded by five halberdiers, splendidly costumed; there were four addi
tional "counsellors," two groups of three seated secretaries and atten
dants, two or three other attendants, and a stage band of six or seve
trumpeters and drummers. At the opening of the scene, drinks were offere
to Claudius and Polonius, who accepted, and to Hamlet and Gertrude, wh
refused. The king rose, so all the court rose. After the king had spoken th
first seven lines as a formal tribute to his late brother, he sat, so all the cour

at. The director was firmly establishing Claudius as the "expert politi-
ian" (to quote his talk to the company), and the court as a splendidly
rganized, smooth-running bureaucratic machine. And in the midst of it,
nprisoned between Claudius and Polonius, self-conscious, intimidated,
nd acutely uncomfortable, was Hamlet. It was an immediate interpreta-
ve emphasis on a Hamlet cowed by political responsibilities.

This image of the court was maintained in later scenes. The play-
ithin-the-play had a large audience. The direction for the opening of Act
hree, Scene Three is, in both the quarto and the Folio, simply "Enter
ing, Rosencrantz, and Guildenstern." Peter Hall had Polonius enter first,
llowed by three counsellors. They sat at a table. The king was accom-
anied by a valet helping him to take off his gown, and those present stood
t his entrance with Rosencrantz and Guildenstern. The king's dispatching
f Rosencrantz and Guildenstern's commission for England thus came to
em far more of an official state action than if it had been performed in
rivate. Similarly in Act Four, Scene Three the opening direction in the
uarto is "Enter King, and two or three," and in the Folio, simply "Enter
ing." In fact, he had five attendants, and he signed papers handed to him
y one of them before he spoke. When Hamlet was brought before the king,
e was under a guard of excessive, if flattering dimensions. Guildenstern,
arrying Hamlet's sword, led him on surrounded by eight halberdiers (or
witzers). As in the first scene, there was something comic and sad about
e discrepancy between the machinery of state and the self-conscious
adequacy of the figure trapped inside it.

In the days when the play of *Hamlet* was identified almost exclusively
ith the character of Prince Hamlet himself, his successor, Fortinbras, was
ften cut from the play altogether. Bernard Shaw's feigned astonishment at
eing his name in the cast list of Forbes-Robertson's production is well-
nown. But as stress has increasingly been laid on the play's political
mension, on the relationships in it between personal and national destiny,
e role has assumed greater importance. Peter Hall omitted only three of
s lines. The direction for his first appearance is another moment when
nakespeare leaves much latitude to his interpreters: "Enter Fortinbras
ith his army over the stage." What is an army? "Three or four ragged
ils," or the hundreds of extras beloved of Victorian presenters of the
story plays? The phrase "over the stage" has been held to imply a
rocessional effect, and Peter Hall had Fortinbras well attended, preceded
y soldiers dragging the cannon, cart, and siege engine, and followed by six
ummers and a number of spearmen. This is lavish for modern times, and
ndoubtedly the director wished Fortinbras to make a strongly martial
pression. Hamlet himself, of course, is disturbedly aware of the contrast

between himself and Fortinbras; their encounter prompts him to the de termination,

from this time forth,
My thoughts be bloody, or be nothing worth! (IV. iv. 65-6).

But is this a good resolution? Peter Hall clearly thought not; his progran note ends with the words: "At the end you are left with Fortinbras, th perfect military ruler. And I don't know about you, but I would nc particularly like to live in Denmark under Fortinbras."

When Peter Hall directed Laurence Olivier as *Coriolanus,* one felt tha the interpretation was being shaped by the actor no less than the directo Indeed, it is interesting that the casting appears to have been the respons bility of the director of the theatre, Glen Byam Shaw, not the director of th production. Harry Andrews has said that Byam Shaw originally intende him to play Coriolanus.[6] But by the time Peter Hall directed *Hamlet,* h could, as director of the theatre, do his own casting. The choice of acto inevitably, of course, has interpretative consequences, and the views of th play's main character that Peter Hall expressed in his talk are closely linke with his choice of actors for these roles, and the way they were playec

Brewster Mason, for example, was ideally suited to embody M Hall's view of Claudius. He is a big man with surprising grace of movemen and gentleness of voice. Some of his best performances have been in majc supporting roles of an avuncular nature, such as Boyet, in *Love's Labour* *Lost,* and Lafeu, in *All's Well That Ends Well.* He can easily exude a blan geniality; his recent Falstaff was praised for this, but he himself admitte that he experienced difficulties with Falstaff's nastier attributes, as in th scene of the stabbing of Hotspur's corpse. Peter Hall had describe Claudius as "a superb operator who hardly ever loses his nerve." Domina ing with his fine presence, Brewster Mason was always in commanc assisted by the deference that his court paid him. In the play scene, fc example, the courtiers waited for his reactions to parts of the play befoi deciding whether to applaud. The most striking break with tradition in th performance was one that emphasized Claudius's self-control and blanc ness. When the climax of the play scene comes, and Claudius can no longe pretend not to notice the parallels between the play and himself, he stoj the performance with a call for lights before leaving: "Give me some ligh Away." Most actors use this as an opportunity for a great histrion moment, a violent eruption of concealed guilt. This Claudius simply stooc glared at Hamlet, and spoke the line with scornful calm, rather rebukii Hamlet for a lapse of taste than showing the depths of his own soul. In curious way, it achieved a *coup-de-théâtre* by denying one.

This stressing of the successful politician in Claudius had its advantages. In a rather perverse essay on the play, Professor Wilson Knight once described Claudius as "the typical kindly uncle."[7] A nephew might have problems in accepting this view of his father's murderer. Brewster Mason was more the uncle than the murderer. Reactions to his performance differed. Some people found his smoothness effectively hateful in itself, but others complained that the character was simplified, that we saw too little of what lay under the smooth surface. There was not enough to suggest the man who could "kill so crudely" (David Benedictus, *The Spectator,* 27 August 1965), whom Hamlet saw as a "satyr," "a mildewed ear," in contrast to his father (Alan Brien, *Sunday Telegraph,* 22 August, 1965), and who might be seen to "suffer from remorse" (*The Times,* 20 August, 1965). The performance was most acceptable to those who could see it as a portrayal of a man with an intellectual rather than an emotional nature, who would act in cold blood, and not be shocked by his own villainy. Thus Robert Speaight, praising Brewster Mason's "very original treatment of 'O my offence,' " described it as a "calm argument of his desperate case," following on appropriately from "his rightly controlled exit from the play."[8]

Some productions of *Hamlet,* especially in the post-Freudian age, have heavily stressed Hamlet's relationship with his mother, perhaps influenced by Ernest Jones's fascinating book, *Hamlet and Oedipus* (London, 1949). Peter Hall reduced her importance in favor of Hamlet's other parent. Elizabeth Spriggs played a Gertrude who was instinctive and acquiescent by nature, warm-hearted but easily swayed, and little troubled by moral considerations. The actress described the character as "a pawn in the game" with no mind of her own (Addenbrooke, p. 130). A little over-dressed, a little vulgar, she was herself vulnerable; she removed a wig while preparing for bed. She was frightened by Hamlet's distress and entirely incapable of understanding what all the fuss was about, but she showed a motherly sympathy for him, and spoke the lines on Ophelia's death with a touching, stunned simplicity. One of the production's more determinedly naturalistic touches was to make her vomit visibly in the scene of her death.

The choice of Glenda Jackson as Ophelia was surprising. With her harsh voice and abrasive personality, she seemed most unlikely to be dominated by her father, or by anyone else. She seemed little less neurotic than Hamlet; indeed, a woman critic (Penelope Gilliatt, *Observer,* 22 August, 1965) suggested that she should have been playing Hamlet: "She makes Ophelia exceptional and electric, with an intelligence that harasses the court and a scornful authority full of Hamlet's own self-distaste. When she says 'Pray you mark' to the twittering Gertrude in the mad scene, she shouts the words as though she could do murder, drumming a heel on the floor and lifting her upper lip in a rictus of contempt.'' And the same critic suggested that perhaps Peter Hall deliberately made her more masculine than usual; that ''when a production places the play so firmly in the world of the cool, politically disaffected generation, one of the first things that will result is a modern blurring of the sexual boundaries.'' That is ingenious; Robert Speaight said, more straightforwardly, that he was not sure what Miss Jackson was getting at. Her harshness suggested sexual neurosis even before the revelations of her sub-conscious mind in the mad scene. A very 'modern,' rebellious personality was portrayed; Peter Hall seems to have been hinting at another young mind twisted by the courtly corruption of Elsinore, even at the expense of our belief that a young woman like this would be as innocently credulous as her first scene, with her brother and father, suggests.

One of the major successes of the production was Tony Church's portrayal of Polonius, though this too could be, and was, accused of going against the text. Peter Hall saw him as ''not a doddering old fool but the kind of shrewd, tough, establishment figure you can still meet in St. James's; a man who sends himself up, and uses his silly humour as a weapon.'' The link between past and present suggested here was also made by reviewers, several of whom spoke of Polonius in terms of a combination of Machiavelli and Harold Macmillan. Mr. Church himself tells me that he had in mind both Lord Burleigh and Mr. Macmillan, chief ministers of the two Elizabeths. The more serious-than-usual interpretation of Polonius at least made Ophelia's respect for him proportionately less surprising. The impression of statesman-like shrewdness was reinforced by the retention of the scene with Reynaldo (II.ii), though the internal cuts — Polonius lost about a third of his lines in this scene — reduced his ramblings and so increased his shrewdness. There were touches of comedy, of course, such as his irritation with both Reynaldo and himself when he lost his thread and could not imagine what he might have meant by ''closes in the consequence.'' But he suggested a very sinister, if unexplained, significance for Polonius's dismissal of Reynaldo: ''Let him ply his music.''

Several critics, while admiring the execution of the role, could not believe that Hamlet would have found it necessary to warn the players not to mock this formidable figure. But Robert Speaight, describing Tony Church's performance as ''the masterpiece among the supporting parts,'' said: ''It has been objected that Polonius is a silly old man, but serious old men are not infrequently silly, and for once we had a Polonius who was the plausible Prime Minister for a pretty unconstitutional monarch. An alert spectator might have noticed that Mr. Church made no apparent sign of overhearing Laertes' last words to Ophelia. Where ninety-nine out of a hundred actors would have obediently 'registered,' Mr. Church merely took down his Machiavelli from the shelf and waited quite a time before he let us know that not a syllable had escaped him.''[9] He is referring to the passage:

> *Laertes* Farewell, Ophelia, and remember well
> What I have said to you.
> *Ophelia* 'Tis in my memory locked,
> And you yourself shall keep the key of it.
> *Laertes* Farewell. *(Exit)*
> *Polonius* What is't, Ophelia, he hath said to you?

This is interesting as an example of how the actor was able simultaneously to suggest a sinister self-control in Polonius and to make a comic point out of it.

I have been speaking of the major supporting roles, and trying to show how the way in which they were played conformed with, and helped to create, the director's personal interpretation of the play. The supporting roles were important in the interpretation, of course; but they were important partly because of the setting they provided for the central character, and of the influences which they suggested as being responsible for his present condition. Undoubtedly the most significant, as also the most controversial, piece of casting was that of David Warner as Hamlet himself. He was only twenty-four years old, and at this time was very much a 'modern,' as opposed to a classical, actor. He was exceptionally tall, but unheroic in build; his face, though expressive, was not conventionally handsome. He did not cultivate grace of movement or beauty of voice, and his verse-speaking was a law unto itself. He had been very successful as Henry VI in Peter Hall's production of *The Wars of the Roses,* and somewhat less successful as Richard II. The roles are significant; both of them rather passive, languid, pathetic characters. To cast him as Hamlet was itself a major interpretative decision. It was obvious that this would be no princely, romantic embodiment of the role. Mr. Warner was, frankly, a gangling, spotty young man with traces of a Midlands accent. No make-up artist would transform him into anything remotely resembling the young Gielgud, and it was clear that Mr. Hall could not wish him to effect such a transformation. His costume and physical appearance seemed clearly designed not just to evoke the student at Wittenberg, but to link him with the modern student. For some of his scenes he wore a student-type gown, and a long, red scarf which seemed strikingly modern in these surroundings.

But Mr. Warner had great audience appeal. For all his height, he had a fragile vulnerability that had made him very touching as Henry VI; the absence in him of actorish mannerisms went some way towards compensating for his technical shortcomings, and was allied with great sensitivity and the ability to convey passionate, if thwarted, sincerity. His 'modern,' classless image had a special appeal for young intellectuals. Interest in the production ran exceptionally high, and it had an unusual amount of advance publicity. Reporters spoke of David Warner as "the youngest Hamlet since Alec Guinness in 1938," and told of rehearsals lasting till six in the morning. Advance booking was heavy, and many people queued all night to buy tickets for the first performance.

One of the pleasures of seeing *Hamlet* repeatedly is to observe the different ways in which directors try to solve the problem of putting a ghost on the stage. Occasionally they evade the problem, as Gielgud did in his New York production of Richard Burton, by representing the Ghost simply by a disembodied voice. Peter Hall's Ghost, on the contrary, was very solid indeed. It was played by an actor standing on a platform inside a machine whose height was variously reported as being anything from eight to twelve feet high. In the lower part of the machine was a stage hand whose duty was to propel it around the stage. It had a "huge artificial head, moveable arms, and a long gown which reached the floor to hide the base-platform and wheeling mechanism which supported it" (Addenbrooke, p. 130). One literal-minded critic complained that in describing the Ghost, Horatio omitted to mention that "the old boy had doubled his height in the underworld" (Alan Brien, *Sunday Telegraph*, 22 August 1965). For the moment of its sudden disappearance (" 'Tis here — 'tis here — 'tis gone") two additional ghosts were used to create a sense of bewildered confusion. When it told Hamlet of the murder, it embraced him, so that the Ghost's plea for revenge and Hamlet's promise to carry it out were spoken with Hamlet cradled in his father's arms. Hamlet wore a miniature painting of his father round his neck, and handled and gazed at it at significant points of the action.

Mr. Warner did much to emphasize Hamlet's nonconformity, his inner rebellion against the Establishment by which he was surrounded. This was a young man who made his own rules and did not mind appearing ridiculous or eccentric. He was making his own discoveries about life, and often enough he found it ridiculous. This was epitomized with a brilliant irony when he tried on the Player's crown to see if it fitted him, and it slipped over his eyes and down his nose, to his evident delight. Even his awkwardness of movement was a symptom of rebellion. Harold Hobson described how he could "stoop from his outrageous height, wave his arms like a scythe, howl to the moon, and go after the King at a most unrefined gallop" *(Sunday Times,* 22 August 1965). In his feigned madness he wore spectacles and a funny hat, lay around on the floor, and wore his cloak "like a belted grey mackintosh" (J. C. Trewin, *Birmingham Post,* 20 August 1965), with his muffler wound around his neck. The eccentricities, the unconventional behavior, brought many accusations of unprinceliness; but some spectators, disregarding the theatre's own conventions, felt that in his very individuality he was truly behaving like a prince. one who had no need to follow convention.

The general impression of this Hamlet was of a disaffected young man, an existentialist drop-out, a beatnik. One critic complained that he did not "seem to have fallen into melancholy as a result of his mother's remarriage; rather he is temperamentally a neurotic intellectual." He could find no consolation outside himself. This sometimes meant playing against the lines, taking them ironically rather than seriously. Hobson remarked that the way he spoke the lines on the "special providence in the fall of a sparrow" suggested that he "cannot bring himself to believe that that providence extends also to him. There are no wings in which he can trust." These lines come towards the opening of the final scene, one of the most interesting in David Warner's interpretation. The duel that follows was very exciting. It was played with proper formality, the court deferential as ever to the king, drums, trumpets and cannonfire marking the ritualistic aspects of the episode. After Laertes made his attack on Hamlet, drawing blood, the duel degenerated into a scuffle. The court closed in and surrounded Hamlet and Laertes in the final stages of their fight. At "The point envenomed too?/ Then, venom, to thy work," Hamlet nicked the king in the neck with terrifying ease, then stabbed him and, as he fell, butted him with his knee, finally sloshing the poisoned drink into his ear, as Claudius had done to Hamlet's father. There was, said the critic of *The Times,* a sense of 'liberated relief," the result of Hamlet's "having finally carried out the Ghost's command without having taken any decision of his own." Fortinbras's approach was heralded with the "warlike noise" of drums and cannonfire, and Hamlet's casting of his "dying voice" to Fortinbras was again spoken against the surface implications, with an ironical suggestion that Hamlet found something comic in the idea either of being succeeded by so different a character, or of a Denmark governed by Fortinbras. One critic put it that Hamlet "giggles when the poison circulates and expires smiling at the thought of the muckup he has bequeathed to Fortinbras" Alan Brien, *Sunday Telegraph,* 22 August 1965). Finally, as he died Hamlet smilingly kissed the miniature of his father that he wore around his neck.

So far, I have been concerned to describe this production rather than to evaluate it. I have had to omit a lot, but I have tried to concentrate on those aspects that were most expressive of the director's point of view. Even though this was not a modern-dress production, a modern view of the play was projected. There is bound, of course, to be a discrepancy between the director's concept and its execution. He, no less than the playwright, has to speak through his interpreters. While David Warner appears to have been very amenable to Peter Hall's direction, his technique was not always adequate to the demands made of it. Many critics complained of a pedantically slow and monotonous delivery of the soliloquies, even suggesting that he was donnish and lectured them at us.

The whole production was felt to be slow; indeed, it is interesting that this performance of a text shorn of about 730 lines lasted only about five minutes less than Mr. Hall's recent production of the complete text, which was criticized for being too rapidly spoken. Mr. Warner had a habit of emphasizing unimportant words and of ending lines on a rising inflection, which could become irritating. But even his speech mannerisms could aid the interpretative effect. John Russell Brown perceptively analysed some of his inflections:

> 'Come to Hecuba,' during the First Actor's Pyrrhus speech, expresses his involvement in the image of a grieving queen and also a weariness with the uses of the world — with Polonius' interference, with the words, with his own involvement; the inflection of the line is reinforced with a movement which is almost comically helpless and weary. When pursued by Rosencrantz, Guildenstern and the officers, his 'Here *they* come' is illuminated with a contemporary inflection that marks 'they' as a composite description of restrictive and uncomprehending authority . . . Later, when the gravedigger displays a skull with 'This same skull, sir, was, sir, Yorick's skull, the King's jester', Hamlet's simple question, 'This?', carries such a shock of precognition — an incipient sense of the need to meet death in personal terms — that the word 'this' seems totally eloquent, a reluctant confrontation of destiny. In these instances David Warner's delivery is so dramatically alive in the use of the simplest verbal means that he challenges many commonly held concepts of Shakespearian 'poetry'.[10]

This is interesting in relation to the production's reception. Initial reactions from both critics and general public included the expression of a certain amount of bewilderment, mixed with disappointment. David Warner was reported to be dissatisfied with his own first-night performance (*Birmingham Mail,* 20 August, 1965). Reviewers of the older generation who had obviously not enjoyed themselves admitted a little uneasily that nevertheless David Warner had clearly appealed to the young people in the audience. "Young people in last night's Stratford audience," wrote Mr. Trewin, "would show, by their overwhelming cheers at the close, that David Warner was the Hamlet of their imagination and their heart. Many of their elders, I think, will hesitate." But other critics, no younger, were immediately enthusiastic. Harold Hobson found the production "better in intellect and emotion than any conventional interpretation one is likely to see for some time" *(Sunday Times,* 22 August 1965). As performances continued, authoritative voices were raised in its defense; Jan Kott wrote a piece in *The Sunday Times* saying he had met many post-graduate students in Cambridge "just like this Hamlet . . . liking to sit on the floor wearing clothes too big for them" and praised a production "in which the equation of modern relevance leaps out of a play's timeless greatness" (31 October 1965). Professor L. C. Knights weighed in on the other channel, in *The Observer,* with the view that it was the best *Hamlet* he had seen, "genuinely moving and highly intelligent."

As performances multiplied, the actors grew in confidence. After it had played 46 times in Stratford, the production moved to the company's London theatre, the Aldwych, where it had another thirty-nine performances, and returned to Stratford in April 1966 to be played sixty-eight more times. It gradually acquired its own orthodoxy. On its return to Stratford John Higgins wrote: "For some years to come, I suspect, David Warner is going to be the yardstick Hamlet. His admirers will judge later interpreters by the light of this compelling, personal and introverted performer; his detractors will remember the shambling figure uttering his lines so dully and praise Hamlets with even a small measure of eloquence and nobility the more warmly for it" *(Financial Times,* 1 May 1966). When it opened, critics had split down the middle; but gradually the word got round, "This was the 'young' *Hamlet* and no one under the age of 25 should utter a word against it." And David Warner was "still playing to a large proportion of under 25s." By now the actors were more confident, the pace had improved, and the long red scarf had been thrown away.

It would seem, then, that Mr. Hall had succeeded at least in his object of finding an image of *Hamlet* that reflected the interests of many people in the 1960s. He had offered a performance that sought to embody ideas about the play that he had expressed in a lecture and in print. In doing so, he had been accused by some critics of going against the text, and of ignoring some aspects of it. He was in several ways in a position similar to that of an academic critic writing an interpretative essay on the play, which might also be subject to accusations of interpretative bias. I am not particularly concerned now with the ethics of theatrical interpretation. Most productions of classic plays reveal a tension between past and present; between, on the one hand, the historical facts about the play's text and its original staging, and, on the other hand, the theatrical and intellectual fashions of the time at which it is being produced. This production projected most of the text of *Hamlet* in ways that related it especially to the intellectual preoccupations of young people in its audiences, and thus achieved yet another theatrical success for the extraordinarily malleable script. What I should like to do in the final part of this talk is to try to relate some aspects of Peter Hall's interpretative emphasis to trends in critical thought about the play, and to suggest how these are related to certain overall patterns of thought in our time.

When, some time ago, I was writing a guide to scholarship and criticism of *Hamlet,* I read within a few months a lot of writings about the play. It seemed to me then that interpretations of it tended to divide according to the view taken of one particular passage. It is part of the dialogue between Hamlet and Horatio shortly before Hamlet is to duel with Laertes, who, we know, intends to bring about Hamlet's death.

Hamlet	I shall win at the odds, but thou wouldst not think how ill all's here about my heart. But it is no matter.
Horatio	Nay, good my lord —
Hamlet	It is but foolery, but it is such a kind of gain giving as would perhaps trouble a woman.
Horatio	If your mind dislike anything, obey it. I will forestall their repair hither and say you are not fit.
Hamlet	Not a whit. We defy augury. There is special providence in the fall of a sparrow. If it be now, 'tis not to come; if it be not to come, it will be now; if it be not now, yet it will come. The readiness is all. Since no man has aught of what he leaves, what is't to leave betimes? Let be. (V.ii.212-225).[11]

A. C. Bradley, in 1904, had indicated two possible ways of taking the passage, while also stating his own preference. "There is," he says, "a trait about which doubt is impossible, — a sense in Hamlet [after his return from England] that he is in the hands of Providence." Citing several passages, including the one that I have quoted, he cannot believe, all the same, "with some critics, that they indicate any material change in his general condition or the formation of any effective resolution to fulfil the appointed duty. On the contrary, they seem to express that kind of religious resignation which, however beautiful in one aspect, really deserves the name of fatalism rather than that of faith in Providence" *(Shakespearean Tragedy* [London, 1904], pp. 144-5). This attitude recurs in later criticism. H. B. Charlton, a confessed disciple of Bradley, puts it more strongly; diagnosing in Hamlet a progressive paralysis ending in despair, he finds in him not "the calm attainment of a higher benignity," but "a fatalist's surrender of his personal responsibility." The "sparrow" speech is "no firm confession of trust in a benign Providence; it is merely the courage of despair" *(Shakespearian Tragedy* [Cambridge, 1949], p. 103). E.M.W. Tillyard, quoting C. S. Lewis and Middleton Murry as critics who have regarded the "sparrow" passage as a sign of

Hamlet's ultimate spiritual regeneration, argues against them. "Quietism not religious enlightenment is the dominating note" *(Shakespeare's Problem Plays* [London, 1950], p. 17). Hamlet is not regenerate; therefore the play is not "tragic in the fullest sense"; therefore he classes it as a "problem play." No less damaging in 1960 was L. C. Knights, who also quotes this passage along with C. S. Lewis's expression of the point of view that Bradley had found it impossible to believe. Lewis had said that Hamlet had lost his way, and that this was "the precise moment at which he finds it again." Knights disagrees; Hamlet represents rather "a corruption of consciousness" which results "in an inability to affirm at all" *(An Approach to 'Hamlet'* [London, 1960], p. 90).

While I was citing some of these judgments on Hamlet, you may have been recalling some of Peter Hall's comments on the play and some of the reviewers' comments on Mr. Warner. Peter Hall spoke of "a terrible fatalism" in Hamlet; Bradley had used the same word. Hall spoke of an "apathy of the will," which may recall Charlton's phrase "a fatalist's surrender of his personal responsibility," or Knights's "inability to affirm at all." Tillyard did not find Hamlet regenerate, and so did not find the play truly tragic; Hall had written: "I don't find *Hamlet* a tragedy in the sense that at the end of it I am left ennobled, purged, and regenerated."

It may seem then that the Hamlet who, according to Harold Hobson, showed in the "sparrow" speech that he "cannot bring himself to believe that that providence extends also to him," who had shied away from responsibility and who died on a giggle, was a logical theatrical projection of a view of the character that had begun to appear in criticism of the play at least sixty years before this production.

It seems to me that this view of the play, growing in force during this century, reflects an intellectual trend that is characteristic of the twentieth century and that may militate against that century's acceptance of part of Shakespeare's meaning. Everyone agrees that the play of *Hamlet* is greatly concerned with the difficulty that a thoughtful man experiences in committing a decisive action. The difficulty of acting is explored in the play partly through the punning metaphor of "acting" in a theatrical sense. The metaphor chosen for self-expression in words is theatrical. The First Player can express in words and gesture his fictional emotion while Hamlet must hold his tongue about his real emotion. Around Hamlet are men who can express themselves spontaneously in action. Laertes reacts immediately and violently to the news of his father's death. The metaphor chosen for self-expression in action is military. The ultimate action is the inflicting of death. The ultimate expression in action of grief for one who has been murdered is revenge by killing; on a larger scale, the ultimate expression of national resentment against an enemy is war: multiple killing. If the action of *Hamlet* is seen as an expanded metaphor, then the deed of killing — judicial or militaristic killing — is the vehicle of the metaphor.

Judicial killing has become increasingly obnoxious to humane people during the twentieth century. So has warfare. It is not easy for us to understand or sympathize with attitudes of mind that condone or encourage them. Mr. Hall's talk to the company strongly implies dissociation from such attitudes; speaking of the apathy of young intellectuals, he said: "You might march against the Bomb. But on the other hand, you might not." The possibility that he did not even think worth stating is that you might march in favor of it. Yet at the beginning, if not at the end, of the First World War, it still seemed to some very civilized people that they could fight the good fight. And indeed even today many people have, however reluctantly, to recognize that this is not necessarily a contradiction in terms.

In Shakespeare's day the difficulty was less. Gentlemen wore swords, and used them. Ben Jonson killed a man in a duel. The idea of taking arms in one's country's interests was generally acceptable; more acceptable than today, simply perhaps because it seemed more directly necessary to self-preservation. Even a young intellectual pacifist of today, I take it, would find it easier to kill someone who had just inflicted a fatal wound on him than to press a button that might kill anonymous masses many miles away. I am not suggesting that Shakespeare lacked humanity, that he was not deeply conscious of the horror of inflicting death, whether on an individual or on an army. He had obviously meditated profoundly on both topics, as *Macbeth* and *Troilus and Cressida* show well enough. Hamlet himself meditates on it. He is inspired by the actors to consider his inadequacies of emotional expression:

> What's Hecuba to him, or he to Hecuba,
> That he should weep for her? What would he do
> Had he the motive and the cue for passion
> That I have? He would drown the stage with tears
> And cleave the general ear with horrid speech . . . (II.ii. 569-73)

In parallel with this, he is inspired by Fortinbras and his army to consider his inadequacies of action:

> Examples gross as earth exhort me.
> Witness this army of such mass and charge,
> Led by a delicate and tender prince,
> Whose spirit, with divine ambition puffed,
> Makes mouths at the invisible event,
> Exposing what is mortal and unsure

> To all that fortune, death, and danger dare,
> Even for an eggshell.

There is a kind of inbuilt illogic in this speech which inevitably suggests that Hamlet is questioning Fortinbras's ethics even while he envies them. Are the lives of Fortinbras and his soldiers really worth no more than an eggshell? This represents perhaps a kind of undertow of doubt in the play which undermines some of its basic premises. Nevertheless, it seems to me, Shakespeare is fundamentally committed to an ethic according to which violent action can be justified by adequate provocation. Hamlet's killing of Polonius and his responsibility for the deaths of Rosencrantz and Guildenstern are apparently condoned. In what seems to me like the kind of moral pointer that Shakespeare occasionally provides when he is uncomfortably aware that his plot has landed him in an awkwardly ambiguous situation, Hamlet defends both his treatment of Rosencrantz and Guildenstern — "Why, man, they did make love to this employment . . ." — and his need to kill the king:

> Does it not, think thee, stand me now upon —
> He that hath killed my king, and whored my mother,
> Popped in between th' election and my hopes,
> Thrown out his angle for my proper life,
> And with such coz'nage — is't not perfect conscience
> To quit him with this arm? And is't not to be damned
> To let this canker of our nature come
> In further evil? (V. ii. 63-70)

Peter Hall cheated, I think, in depriving Hamlet of his last sentence here, the defence that in killing the king he will be removing a cancer, thus fulfilling the destiny that he had previously regretted:

> The time is out of joint. O cursèd spite
> That ever I was born to set it right.

If we grant this, we can, I think, see a Hamlet who finally does affirm, who acts positively for good ends, who can hope to have done the state some service, a Hamlet whose contemplation of death has matured into an acceptance of the demands of life as well as the fact of death, who accepts providence as an inscrutable but trustworthy guide to right behavior. The man who removes a cancer is on the side of life, not of death; he is not apathetic, but positively, valuably active. If this had been the vehicle of Shakespeare's metaphor, not just a metaphor within a metaphor, we should find the play easier to accept on its own terms. If Claudius were literally a cancer, and Hamlet a surgeon having problems in coming to terms with the need to commit major surgery to remove it, the play would be more acceptable to modern times, and we should not wish him to be apathetic. In shying away from the metaphor that Shakespeare has expanded to construct the action of the play, we distort the play.

The critics who represent the viewpoint expressed by Peter Hall find something falsely romantic in those who support the belief that Hamlet is finally successful because he kills the king. They would not feel this, I think, if his success was to cure a mortally sick patient. If we could accept Shakespeare's story as a metaphor as well as an imitation of an action, we might more easily endorse Horatio's epitaph on Hamlet: "Now cracks" — not an immature, not a fatalistic, not an apathetic, but — "a noble heart."

FOOTNOTES

1. David Addenbrooke, *The Royal Shakespeare Company* (London, 1974), p. 129.

2. *Characters of Shakespeare's Plays*, 1817 (World's Classics, London, 1916, etc.), p. 86.

3. Absolute accuracy in these figures is not possible because of the amount of prose in the play, and because some of the cuts are of phrases within lines.

4. Figures are given by Claris Glick in her article *"Hamlet* in the English Theater — Acting Texts from Betterton (1676) to Olivier (1963),"* *Shakespeare Quarterly* 20:1 (Winter, 1969), 17-35.

5. *Preface* (1765), in *Johnson on Shakespeare,* edited by Walter Raleigh (London, 1908, etc.), p. 22.

6. Interview with Harry Andrews in *Olivier,* edited by Logan Gourlay (London, 1973), pp. 77-8.

7. "The Embassy of Death: An Essay on *Hamlet,"* in *The Wheel of Fire* (London, 1930), pp. 34-50, 37.

8. "Shakespeare in Britain," *Shakespeare Quarterly* 17:4 (Autumn, 1966), 389-98, 396.

9. "Shakespeare in Britain," *Shakespeare Quarterly* 16:4 (Autumn, 1965), 314-24, 322.

10. "The Royal Shakespeare Company 1975," *Shakespeare Survey* 19 (1970), pp. 111-118, 113.

11. It is a misfortune that there is serious doubt about what Shakespeare actually wrote as the penultimate sentence. I follow the prompt-book for 1965, which represents a reversion from the Signet text used for Hall's production to Rowe's 1709 version of the Folio reading.

III

John Barton's *Twelfth Night,* 1969-72

Judi Dench as Viola and Donald Sinden as Malvolio. Photograph by Joe Cocks.

Hamlet is one of the most controversial of Shakespeare's plays. It has been endlessly discussed, and poses major interpretative problems. *Twelfth Night* has provoked less dissension. As with many of the comedies, there is general agreement about the broad lines along which the play should be interpreted. Disputes are about matters of balance, emphasis, and degree, especially about the balance between comedy and seriousness. To what extent, if at all, should Orsino be satirically presented? Should Feste be primarily an entertainer, or should the actor suggest in him the sadness attributed to those possessed of perfect knowledge? Should the portrayal of Olivia emphasize the aristocratic head of a household or the susceptible young girl? And, perhaps most dominant in the questions asked about the play's characters, how seriously should we take Malvolio's plight? Is it right that he should create, as, 150 years ago, Charles Lamb said that Bensley created, a "kind of tragic interest?"[1] Or should the performance be cooler, more distanced, more critical? More general interpretative questions that might be asked about the play concern the balance in it of romance and realism, of idealized love and drunken revelry, of wise folly and foolish wit, of self-control and relaxation, of love songs and songs of good life.

In 1958 Peter Hall had directed this play at Stratford with great success. He had an exquisite Viola in Dorothy Tutin, and the production was visually very beautiful. Interpretatively it was notable for two performances at opposite ends of the spectrum, as it were. Geraldine McEwan played Olivia in a style that broke away entirely from the tradition of presenting her as a serious, somewhat matronly young mistress of a household, and showed her instead as a rather silly, giggly, flirtatious, and very pretty young girl. Feste, on the other hand, as played by both Cyril Luckham and Max Adrian was distinctly melancholy, an elderly fool in great danger of losing his job, and of deserving to do so, grieving rather than mirthful about the trick played on Malvolio. This production was revived in 1960. I saw it a dozen or more times, and regarded it as a classic, especially in its realization of the play's more romantic qualities.

It was certainly not eclipsed for me by the following Stratford production, by Clifford Williams in 1966. Diana Rigg was charming as Viola, but this was a light-weight version, skating over many of the play's more serious issues, and with some frivolities that seemed merely silly. Orsino was more critically presented by Alan Howard than by any other actor I have seen. Vanity and affectation emerged as his dominant characteristics. David Warner's humorous pathos came into its own in the role of Sir Andrew Aguecheek, but the production did not engrave itself deeply upon the memory.

Throughout Peter Hall's directorate of the Stratford theatre, he worked closely with his former fellow-student at Cambridge, John Barton. They collaborated in a production of *Troilus and Cressida* in 1960, and in 1963 of *The Wars of the Roses*, versions of Shakespeare's *Henry VI* and *Richard III*, for which Mr. Barton wrote what would have been referred to in film circles as the "additional dialogue" — over a thousand lines of it. Shakespeare's other tetralogy of English history plays was added in 1964, to form a great historical cycle with which the company celebrated the four-hundredth anniversary of Shakespeare's birth. Mr. Barton was also responsible for independent productions of *The Taming of the Shrew* (1960), *Love's Labour's Lost* (1965), *Coriolanus* (1967), *All's Well That Ends Well* (1967), *Julius Caesar* (1968), and *Troilus and Cressida* (1968). In 1968 Peter Hall resigned his directorate and was succeeded by Trevor Nunn. For 1969 Mr. Nunn devised a season which concentrated on late plays by Shakespeare: *Pericles, The Winter's Tale,* and *Henry VIII.* He also invited John Barton to direct *Twelfth Night.* It is this production on which I wish to concentrate today. It was played thirty times at Stratford in 1969. In 1970 it was given forty performances in Australia and forty-seven at the Aldwych Theatre in London. It returned to Stratford in the following year for another seventy-one performances, and in 1972 was given fourteen times in Japan. This adds up to a total of 202 performances. Inevitably, there were cast changes from time to time. Three different actors played Sir Toby Belch and Sebastian; two different performers played each of Malvolio, Sir Andrew Aguecheek, Orsino, Fabian, and Maria. Among the leading roles, Feste, Olivia, and Viola remained constant throughout. I saw the production several times during each of its Stratford seasons, and it came to impress itself even more deeply on my imagination than Peter Hall's. The prompt-books for both 1969 and 1971 are missing, but I have been able to consult the one used at the Aldwych in 1970, and also that used for the Japanese tour in 1972.

John Barton once said in an interview: "I never feel satisfied with a production of mine when it first opens. We rehearse for six and a half weeks, which really isn't long for a full-scale production of a complex play . . . Work has only reached a certain point when rehearsals come to an end. One of the advantages of the Royal Shakespeare Company is that we can keep a play in the repertoire for another year, or more; almost invariably, this develops the production" *(Plays and Players,* November, 1969). Mr. Barton's production of *Twelfth Night* changed and developed during its repeated performances and its variations of cast, though many of the changes were of the kind that result from improvements in timing or the scarcely definable differences created by an actor's personality, voice, and appearance, even when he is dressed in the same costumes as his predecessor in a role, and is using similar gestures, movements, and stage business. The production was refined in some ways, but remained relatively constant in its objectives throughout its run. To attempt a thorough discrimination among its various phases would be beyond my powers; more important, it would be boring. Memories have blended, and my account will at many points be a composite one.

In the interview from which I have quoted, given only a few months after the *Twelfth Night* had opened, Mr. Barton spoke about his aims in directing it: "The text is so familiar, I think, to everyone that there is a danger of staleness. I suppose I started out with the idea that the play should as far as possible emerge uncluttered: free from previous conceptions, clichés, traditional interpretations of specific characters or scenes. I issued a caveat to the cast at the start of rehearsals against 'business,' — *Twelfth Night* seems to have a tendency to accrue excessive business at many points. And I tried to avoid imposing an ostentatious directional hand: it is very much an actors' play. The text contains an enormous range of emotions and moods and most productions seem to select one — farce or bitterness or romance — and emphasize it throughout. I wanted to sound all the notes that are there."

In several ways this is an admirable expression of intent. It shows an awareness of the dangers of theatre tradition, the need to rethink the script from the beginning, which is one of most valuable characteristics of the post-war generation of university-trained directors. It shows an awareness too that the application of "an ostentatious directional hand" is likely to reduce and limit a play's emotional range. It is, we may observe, a general statement, one which might equally apply to many plays. In this it is characteristic of Mr. Barton. He dislikes making theoretical statements about plays. He has an inquiring, probing, exploratory mind that does not easily express itself in categorical statements. Something of this is evident in the remarks made in the same interview about his approach to rehearsing a play.

> I probably do less background reading for a production, of critical or historical material, than most of my colleagues. I much prefer to immerse myself in the text itself, until I know it backwards. I also do very little by way of detailed critical exposition of a play. In fact I can't do it. I start rehearsals with certain feelings and ideas about the play, but without a detailed overall interpretation. Rather than defining, legislating, or making intellectual generalizations, I prefer to begin, if possible, by responding to what the actor provides. I like to set basic moves, to get them to learn the text as soon as possible, and then dig deeply into it: working on stress, inflexion, pitching and phrasing of the surface of the verse, and through these things to the mood, the intentions, the contradictions, and the living breath of feeling underneath.

The emphasis on the text here is a pointer to one of John Barton's greatest skills as a director; that is, the capacity to train his actors to deliver verse with a sensitivity to its full potential range of meaning, both intellectual and emotional. Many of the leading actors of the company have expressed, sometimes in talking to our students from Furman, their admiration and gratitude for his work with them on the speaking of verse. The empiricism suggested in Mr. Barton's remarks is undoubtedly part of his makeup, but it should not be misconstrued as a lack of true engagement with the text. The final result of his methods, in his best productions, is far from a negative one. As we shall see in examining his *Twelfth Night* and, still more emphatically, his *Richard II,* what ultimately emerges is a genuine and positive interpretation.

Mr. Barton is the most highly-trained, academically, of our directors. He did graduate research in Elizabethan drama at King's College, Cambridge, where he was for six years the lay-dean. He was over thirty years old before he became a full-time professional man of the theatre. Nevertheless, his approach is not in any pejorative sense academic. He has written that the director is "engaged in an act of critical interpretation analogous to that undertaken by the literary critic in his study."[2] But he prefers — wisely, it seems to me — to let the interpretation emerge from the performance rather than to formulate it in critical statements. One result of this is a reluctance to write notes to be printed in the programs of the productions for which he is responsible. However, Mr. Barton is married to a Shakespeare scholar and critic of great distinction. As Anne Righter, she wrote *Shakespeare and the Idea of the Play* (1962, etc.), which has become a classic of modern Shakespeare criticism; she edited *The Tempest* for the New Penguin Shakespeare; and she has written the Introductions to the comedies in the Riverside edition. The program for her husband's production of *Twelfth Night* includes a note by her which undoubtedly he approved, and which may be taken, I think, as reflecting some of his own views on the play. Mrs. Barton later developed some of the ideas first expressed in her note in a fine essay, "*As You Like It* and *Twelfth Night:* Shakespeare's Sense of an Ending."[3]

Her note draws attention to the central position of this play in Shakespeare's career. It is the last of his Elizabethan comedies, and employs many of the conventions and themes that he had explored in the nine comedies preceding it. At the same time, it "prefigures the final romances." This, of course, is true; it is also appropriately noted in a season during which *Pericles* and *The Winter's Tale* were to be performed. Mrs. Barton points out that Viola accepts her strange situation rather than tries to transform it, as Julia and Rosalind had, and that she puts her faith "in the mysterious symmetries of a universe whose 'tempests are kind, and salt waves fresh in love'." She points to the associations of the play's title with a period of revelry, "a feast at which the world turned upside down, pleasure became a kind of obligation, and ordinary rules of conduct were reversed." All the characters of the play are in abnormal states of mind except for Malvolio, who alone tries to check "this abdication from commonsense," and so becomes the general enemy. But holiday is not eternal. In the last act of the play, "fantasy fights against the cold light of day." Admittedly, some characters — Viola, Orsino, Olivia and Sebastian — recover their sanity, gain in self-knowledge, but also "remain privileged inhabitants of Illyria . . . where people are shipwrecked into good fortune, and the dead return." But the others are "exiled into reality." They cannot "be absorbed into the harmony of the romantic plot," and "are not even allowed to remain on stage with the happy lovers at the end." The audience too at the end of the play "faces its own jolt into reality, but at least it is given Feste and not Malvolio as its guide." He sings his poignant last song, dismissing us "to a world beyond holiday, where 'the rain it raineth every day'."

As a critical statement this is, of course, fairly generalized; and it points, with complete justification, to certain forces in the play's language, such as Viola's statement that if her particular desire is granted — if, that is, Sebastian is alive — then she can believe the general, though paradoxical, proposition that "tempests are kind, and salt waves fresh in love." Mrs. Barton's emphasis on madness is the result partly of the application to the play of historical knowledge about Twelfth-night customs, partly of a perception about the play's language. Her comments on the ending again attribute symbolical, generalizing significance to the stage action: it is microcosmic, emblematic of truths about illusion and reality. We shall see that the production went some way, at least, towards embodying these ideas in sound and action.

Anyone who has taught Shakespeare to young people who have little or no experience of seeing his plays performed will agree, I think, that it is much more difficult to bring comedy, especially verbal and poetic comedy, to life in the classroom than to show the power of strong drama or tragedy. Even Falstaff can fall devastatingly flat before children, who find his language difficult and who lack the assistance afforded by stage picture and physical presence. The teacher's problem is akin to that of the director. He too has to breathe life into the words, to create a superstructure of interpretative movement, facial and gestural expression, physical relationship of characters, vocal inflection, and visual setting which will attempt to realize the full potential of the playwright's words. He has to give a play the unwritten dimension imagined but not fully realized by its author, and inevitably this dimension differs each time the play is produced. To some extent he is obeying instructions that may be explicit in the stage directions — though in Shakespeare these are often scanty — or implicit in the words spoken. But much is left entirely to the discretion of the director and his actors. I should like to consider some of the ways in which John Barton filled out the text of *Twelfth Night,* realizing its harmonies in the attempt, as he put it, to "sound all the notes that are there."

For the previous plays in the season's repertory, the setting had been a large, white, box-like structure which lined the stage. For *Twelfth Night* the designer, Christopher Morley, placed inside this "a long receding wattle tunnel decorated by four stately, flickering candlesticks, but lit from the outside, sometimes a sombre twilight umber, sometimes soaring into sunburst brilliance" (J. W. Lambert, *The Sunday Times,* 24 August 1969). Doors at the back of the tunnel could open to reveal suggestions of a garden or the city. The set was restful on the eye, and some beautiful stage pictures were created. Particularized settings were indicated by changes of lighting, sound effects, and furniture, all of it silvery-white: an elegant garden table and chairs, a deckchair, a sundial, a trellis-screen, stylized trees and a box hedge. Costumes were Jacobean in style and subdued in coloring, such as the olive-green suit worn by Viola as Cesario, and the light brown and dark red of Olivia's dress when she had given up her mourning.

Sound effects were of great importance. Some were relatively simple. Bird song, along with sunny lighting, helped to establish the daytime, open-air setting for a number of scenes; a different bird, the owl, impressed on us that the revelling of Sir Toby and his fellows was a nocturnal activity. Other sounds were more resonantly symbolic. In the later part of the play, for example, Olivia was several times associated with the sound of chiming bells. They were first heard in response to an authoritative stage direction when, while she is talking to Cesario of her love for him, she says (more truly than she knows) "The clock upbraids me with a waste of time" (III. ii. 132). They sounded again in the last scene, less realistically, at her entrance. During Sebastian's soliloquy expressing his wonder and rapture at Olivia's acceptance of him, the cries of the imprisoned Malvolio, witnessed in the previous scene, were twice distinctly heard, once when Sebastian said, "This may be some error, but no madness," and again at his declaration that he was willing to deny the evidence of his senses that either he or Olivia was mad. Thus the idea of the questioning of the boundaries between sanity and madness, raised in Mrs. Barton's program note, was underlined by the director. More powerful and evocative still was a recording of the sound of waves beating upon a sea-shore, and of the cries of sea-birds, which, along with modulations in the lighting which made transparent and luminous the wicker walls of the stage set, opened up our imaginations to a sense of a world elsewhere, a mysteriously benevolent providence associated with the sea, with the possibility that "Tempests are kind, and salt waves fresh in love." Mrs. Barton had drawn attention to this line, and anyone familiar with the criticism of G. Wilson Knight will know that it marks a direct prefigura-tion of the dominant imagery of Shakespeare's last plays. This kind of theatrical symbolism may seem excessive in its nudging of the audience into attributing special significance to particular passages, providing directional footnotes, as it were; and there were one or two complaints of heavy-handedness. Personally I found it an acceptable and unobtrusive comple-ment to the verbal imagery, a poetic way of directing a poetic play.

Few of Shakespeare's comedies mingle romantic seriousness with com-edy as successfully as *Twelfth Night,* and one of the finest qualities of Mr. Barton's production was his preservation of this fusion of tones. It will be convenient for my purposes to emphasize first the ways in which he brought out the play's comedy, and then those in which he deepened its seriousness. Yet often the two aims were indivisible. Of course, much of the comedy of Viola derives from the ironies in her situation as a girl disguised as a boy, and these were humorously pointed. Judi Dench is one of our best performers of romantic comedy. She has a very feminine beauty and tenderness, a clear, bright voice, and a sense of fun that communicates itself through a virtuosic skill in timing. Viola's femininity was cleverly stressed on her first entry, before she dons her disguise. Led by the sea-captain and followed by two stalwart sailors, she emerged through the back doors to sounds of the sea amid wafts of smoke suggestive of sea-spray. Long, fair hair hung down almost to her waist; there was a touch of Alice in Wonderland in her appearance as she looked wonderingly about her and asked: "What country, friends, is this?" But in disguise, with cropped hair and a nicely cultivated swagger, she was admirably boyish.

Some bits of business were devised to enhance the comic irony. When she first appeared at court, Valentine, congratulating Cesario on the Duke's favors, disconcertingly slapped her on the bosom; moments later, when the Duke had entered, he pointed to a stool and pulled it close to him, indicating that Cesario should sit on it; she pulled it away before sitting down; he pulled it back to him. The actress's momentary flinchings, signs of nervousness that would be understandable in a boy newly promoted to favor at court, held an extra dimension of meaning for those who knew the boy was a girl; and so a bond of complicity was entered into with the audience. Left onstage at the end of the scene, she could reveal to us her sympathetic amusement at her own situation: "Whoe'er I woo, myself would be his wife." There was intelligent irony as well as wistfulness in the delivery of the line, showing us Viola's independent resilience as well as her affectionate nature. In her next scene with the Duke, we were given an initial reminder of the true situation as he pulled her stool towards him and held on to her to prevent her moving away, but the scene was played for its full emotional power. Judi Dench spoke her lines about "Patience on a monument" with a quietly beautiful intensity, and late in the scene there came a brilliant fusion of a comic apprehension of an irony with a sense of deep emotion. "But died thy sister of her love, my boy?" asked Orsino. "I am all the daughters of my father's house, / And all the brothers, too . . ." replied Cesario; and a tiny pause followed by a catch in the voice as she said "brothers" took us movingly from the fictional situation of Viola speaking equivocally to conceal her own disguise, to the reality of the situation in which she genuinely believed that she had lost her brother. This was truly poetic acting.

Shakespeare swings the balance back to the comic in the scene (III.i) in which Olivia tells Cesario of her love for him. Sitting in embarrassingly close proximity to Olivia on a double seat, Judi Dench dealt with the situation with great comic tact, suggesting rueful sympathy with the unfortunate Olivia along with a humorous embarrassment at her own plight. Her sure comic touch was also brilliantly displayed in the mock duel with Sir Andrew.

At its most verbal Shakespeare's comedy requires little in the way of directional invention to make its effect. But in some episodes of his plays he leaves a good deal to his performers. There are scenes in which the comedy is largely dependent on action and movement; an obvious, rather extreme example is the episode of the wrestling match in *As You Like It*. In *Twelfth Night,* such a scene is Act Two, Scene Three, the episode of drunken revelry which is interrupted by the entrance of the outraged Malvolio. John Barton built this up carefully, with a number of individual touches. For example, Feste's first words after he has entered are "How now, my hearts. Did you never see the picture of 'we three'?" It is a line that needs a scholarly note; the traditional explanation is that a picture of "we three" is "a sign-board representing two fools or two ass-heads and inscribed 'we three,' the spectator being the third" (New Cambridge edition; see also M. M. Mahood's note in the New Penguin edition). This would be difficult to convey to a modern audience; Mr. Barton ingeniously found a way of illustrating the line that was meaningful and humorous; simultaneously Feste clapped a hand to his eyes, Sir Andrew covered his mouth, and Sir Toby put his hands over his ears. They held the pose for a moment, recalling the traditional emblem of the three monkeys, "See no evil, hear no evil, speak no evil." The fun came partly from the immediacy of the response; there was a suggestion of a long-familiar, often-repeated comic routine, a kind of family joke which had become funnier by long repetition; and in this way the moment contributed to the impression of a shared background among the members of Olivia's household. This is something that John Barton was careful to develop. It is a subtle and difficult matter. Too often in the theatre it would be only too easy to believe that characters who have supposedly grown up together have only just been introduced to one another. In this production the sense of a remembered past was strong. It emerged again, touchingly, while Feste sang "O mistress mine" to Sir Toby and Sir Andrew. The song was clearly one that the three men had often enjoyed together. Sir Andrew and Sir Toby hummed along with him in the second verse, and Feste continued to hum the melody as they made their comments. The sentiment was a little alcoholic, perhaps, but nonetheless touching.

Music, of course, plays a major part in this scene and, indeed, throughout the play. One of the director's methods of articulating the scenes was to have Feste come on ahead, or linger behind, accompanying himself on his lute as he sang a phrase from one of his songs; often the words formed an oblique comment on the situation. Sir Andrew had been revealed in his earlier scene to have musical talents unsuspected by previous performers in the role. Perhaps taking his Christian name as a cue, John Barton made him a Scotsman. A Scotsman is, of course, most easily identified by his kilt. This Sir Andrew wore only a Jacobean approximation to one, but he had a sporran. Moved by Sir Toby's generosity to Feste, he foraged deep inside it, and, showing great consciousness of self-sacrifice, parted with a small, a very small, coin. The prompter's note instructs Feste to "kill moths." Still more Scottishly, this Sir Andrew played bagpipes. The bagpipes, indeed, became something of a joke of the Stratford season. Not many Shakespeare productions call for bagpipes; but the property room found a pair that had been played, not by Laurence Olivier as Macbeth, but by Peter O'Toole as Petruchio. Ability to play this instrument is not normally required of recruits to the Royal Shakespeare Company. But actors are versatile; a tutor was found; he was a pipemaster; it was alleged to be only a coincidence that his name was Bob Shakespeare. Weird noises emanated from the dressing-rooms during rehearsals; it was reported that practice sessions were held on a boat moored in the middle of the river.

The bagpipes contributed, of course, to the scene of revelry. After Feste has sung "O mistress mine," Sir Toby calls for a catch, and Maria joins the party. Now Sir Andrew could really show his musical talent. The clowns sang more than is set down for them — legitimately enough in this scene. Sir Toby's description of Malvolio as a "Peg-a-Ramsey" was the cue for a four-line song, "Peggy is a Bonny Lass," and his "There dwelt a man in Babylon" was taken further than the lines set down by Shakespeare. The old ballad to which he alludes continues:

> Of reputation great in fame;
> He took to wife a fair woman;
> Susanna was her name.

But here the name was varied to Maria; the episode became a kind of mock-courtship of Maria, who stood on a chair as the revellers danced around her. Complexities of emotion emerged. The mock-courtship by Sir Toby was something in which Maria would have liked to believe; a clasp of hands between Feste and her suggested a sympathetic understanding between them. In this episode the bagpipes came into their own. "O' the twelfth day of December," too, was extended, and the words of the well-known Christmas song were sung in full, and repeated with bagpipe accompaniment. With every justification, the director was building on the hints in the text to mount to a climax of uninhibited mirth that would be interrupted by the entrance of the repressive Malvolio. When the merriment was at its height, he entered, glared at the revellers, at first unseen by them, and wrapped his cloak around his neck in an angry but ludicrous movement. Jollity subsided. Sir Toby sat, and Sir Andrew lay, half-stretched on the ground. "My masters, are you mad?" barked Malvolio. Sir Andrew subsided further, accidentally blowing the last breath of air from his bagpipes in what sounded like a final derisory squeak.

Sir Andrew is a character whose comedy comes from foolishness

Exploited by Sir Toby and ridiculous in his aspirations to Olivia, he provides opportunities which are attractive to actors, and he has frequently been played by actors of higher status than the size of the role might appear to warrant. At Stratford over the last twenty years, for example, the role had been taken by Richard Johnson, Ian Richardson, and David Warner. In 1969 Barrie Ingham, who was playing Leontes in the same season, was Sir Andrew. The role is one in which comedy and pathos are often inseparable, because the pathos comes from a realization of inadequacy which also has comic aspects. John Barton and Barrie Ingham found a number of ways of reinforcing this area of the role. Sir Andrew was played as an eager innocent, inexperienced and kind-hearted. Maria was something of a mother-figure. After Sir Toby had rebuffed her, on the line, "'Tis too late to go to bed now," Sir Andrew took her hand and kissed it with a compassionate attempt at gallantry. He was easily shocked; when he overheard Malvolio commenting on the handwriting of the letter supposedly from Olivia, he asked Sir Toby and Fabian: "Her c's, her u's, and her t's: why that?" The line has, of course, obscene implications, and the prompt book reads: "They tell him. Aguecheek shocked is pulled down." He carried a posy of flowers ready to present to Olivia should the opportunity arise; a reviewer reported: "When he hears that Olivia cannot abide anything yellow he quietly and sadly conceals the little bunch of primroses with which he has been hoping to woo her, and thereafter carries only pink flowers" (*Glasgow Herald,* 25 August 1969). When at last he found himself in Olivia's presence, he offered her the flowers, but was rewarded by no more than a bow, and was so distressed that he had to be pulled away by Maria. In general, though the comic side of Sir Andrew was not neglected, the pathetic was emphasized.

The most important comic figure of the play is, I suppose, Malvolio, who was played initially by Donald Sinden, one of our most brilliant comic actors. A tall and commanding figure, he was made-up in a way that suggested Malvolio's repressive nature, like "a Victorian cartoon Humpty Dumpty, all bald, ruffed and painfully etched sneer lines, with spindly legs disappearing into baggy, emasculated-looking breeches" (Ronald Bryden, *Observer*, 24 August 1969). His first appearance stressed his pomp of office. Before this, at the end of the second scene, he led a little procession of Olivia and members of her household, dressed in mourning, across the stage as if to a religious service, providing a visual cue for Sir Toby's first line: "What a plague means my niece to take the death of her brother thus?" He carried a staff of office, which became a symbol of his love of authority; he banged it on the floor to signal Olivia's entry and before issuing commands.

Several reviewers remarked on the laughter he provided merely by the way he spoke his first word. "What think you of this fool, Malvolio? doth he not mend?'' Olivia asks. ''Yes,'' he replies; and Donald Sinden contrived, by the skill of his timing, facial expression, and inflection to suggest a height of contemptuous superiority that gathered together and released in laughter the amusement that the audience had increasingly been feeling at his uncomfortable presence. He bullied Maria, obviously trying to keep her severely in her place. But he was deferential to his mistress. ''Run after that same peevish messenger,'' she says, telling him to return Orsino's ring to Cesario. ''Run?'' Malvolio echoed, in a directorial addition suggesting that for at least the last twenty years he had not proceeded at any but the most stately pace. Nevertheless, after she had finished speaking he hitched up his cloak, balanced his staff in his hand, and propelled himself into a kind of slow-motion canter, aptly described by Ronald Bryden as a ''Zulu lope,'' which was very funny.

John Barton, like Peter Hall before him, placed Act Two, Scene Two before Act Two, Scene One, so that Malvolio's exit in search of Cesario is almost immediately followed by his re-entrance behind ''him.'' Malvolio had placed the ring which he is to give to Cesario on his finger, and began to take it off with the words: ''She returns this ring to you, sir.'' The ring stuck, so he continued: ''You might have saved me my pains, to have taken it away yourself.'' He pulled again at the ring, unsuccessfully, so continued: ''She adds, moreover, that you should put your lord into a desperate assurance she will none of him.'' Another tug; still it would not move: ''And one thing more, that you be never so hardy to come again in his affairs'' — success at last — ''unless it be to report your lord's taking of this . . .'' The tenacity with which Malvolio refused to accept defeat, his humorless insistence that he had to go on talking, seemed to me a brilliant and original reading of the speech. As he departed he involuntarily burst into his run again, but pulled himself together and resumed his normal gait as he realized that this was no longer necessary.

More inventive touches came in the handling of the letter-scene. The line of verse, ''M O A I doth sway my life,'' is not fully understood, but Donald Sinden made it comic by running the letters together and pronouncing them as a sort of feline wail; puzzling over them later he read: ''Softly! M, comma, O, comma,'' etc. A sundial was on stage for the scene in which he comes, in his yellow cross-garters, into Olivia's presence; as *Punch* put it: ''So confident is he now of his future greatness that when he glances down from his watch to the sundial he has been honoring with his elbow it is the sundial he alters, shifting it bodily through thirty degrees'' (Jeremy Kingston, 19 August 1970). As I record these comic touches, I am aware of the inadequacy of my reporting. One can say objectively what happened; but only a writer with a genius for comic description equal to the genius of the actor who performed the role could convey a sense of the effect of what was done.

I have implied already that the comedy of this production was often shot through, perhaps even intensified, by sadness. Having sketched some of the ways in which the comedy was heightened, I should like now to try to point to ways in which the fundamental seriousness of the play was made manifest. *Twelfth Night* is profoundly concerned with human relationships. Part of the sadness underlying the play derives from the fact that many of these are unfulfilled, thwarted, or unreciprocated. Sir Andrew's feeble attempts to court Olivia exemplify this. He is a sadly unrelated character, waving feebly as he drowns. Even with Sir Toby's encouragement, he is timid and gauche in his encounter, early in the play, with Maria; and he seems never even to have been introduced to Olivia. Also unsatisfactory, though in ways that are not made fully explicit, is his relationship with Sir Toby. There are several hints that Sir Toby is a parasite on him. Like Falstaff, Toby is a morally ambiguous figure. As the main upholder of revelry in the play, he is naturally sympathetic. He was played in this production as a gentleman, albeit a rather seedy one. There was about him a hint of the retired army officer. When Tony Church played the role, he made a powerful moment of his major confrontation with Malvolio. His lines, "Art any more than a steward? Dost thou think because thou art virtuous, there shall be no more cakes and ale?" were spoken with a passion that was the more impressive because it was clear from Maria's reactions that in thus challenging Malvolio he was endangering his own place in Olivia's household. This was one of the ways in which the play's economic realities were brought home to us. It revealed a hard capacity for anger in Sir Toby, not just a genial desire to defend the pleasure principle. And this anger was apparent in his last appearance. Entering, drunk, with Feste and Maria, whose presence is not required by the text, he collided with Orsino, and bowed in apology. The sense of consternation among the onlookers was increased by the omission of Olivia's decisive: "Away with him!" Sir Toby's rejection of Andrew's well-meant offer of help was fierce and bitter: "Will you help? an ass-head, and a coxcomb, and a knave? a thin-faced knave, a gull!" It was followed by a long pause, giving Andrew an opportunity to register his disillusionment, before Sir Toby was helped off by his new wife, with a disconsolate Sir Andrew, pathetically offering a final bow to Olivia, bringing up the rear.

Another unsatisfactory relationship in the play is that between Sir Toby and Maria. Scholarship has stressed that she should be a gentlewoman, not a serving-maid, as she used to be played. Both actresses who played the part in this production were mature women, looking almost old enough to be Olivia's mother. Understandably, Sir Toby's line, "Look, where the youngest wren of nine comes" (III.ii. 64-5), was omitted. The clue to the way in which the role was played obviously derived from the final piece of information we are given about Maria — that Sir Toby, as a recompense for her having written, at his great importunity, the letter by which Malvolio was tricked, has married her. The phrasing suggests both reluctance on her part to write the letter and a desire to be married to Sir Toby, and these clues were picked up and read backwards into the play's sub-text, as it were.

The two actresses cast as Maria are of very different temperaments. Brenda Bruce played her as a cheerful, even mischievous woman of some worldly experience, whose slightly coarse jollity compensated for a disillusioned realistic underlying sadness. Elizabeth Spriggs, wearing steel-rimmed spectacles and adopting a genteel Scottish accent, prim of manner and innocent in expression, suggested rather a repressed governess. This made her behavior in the encounter with Sir Andrew, when she has to apply his hand to her bosom — "I pray you, bring your hand to th' buttery-bar, and let it drink" (I.iii. 71-2) — less than credible. But both performances were admirably executed in their different ways, and both suggested a rather sad realization on Maria's part that, whatever Sir Toby's faults, she stood no chance of winning a more eligible husband. Maria cared for Sir Toby; in their first scene, as she rebuked him for his "ill hours," she bustled around bringing him food and, in a businesslike way, came behind him, held his nose so that he opened his mouth, and then poured down his throat what was doubtless some potent but obnoxious cure for a hangover, while continuing to talk to him. She put up with rudeness from him. An interpretative gloss was given to Sir Toby's last line in the night scene. Maria has left, with the words: "For this night, to bed, and dream on the event." She tried to take Sir Toby's hand to lead him away, but he rejected her. She went sadly behind a screen. No re-entry is required, but she came from behind the screen as Sir Toby said, "Come, come, I'll go burn some sack," and tried again to lead him away. His words, "'Tis too late to go to bed now," were addressed to her, and he was clearly rejecting her favors as he pushed her away. After he had gone, Sir Andrew sympathetically kissed her hand, and Feste rounded off the scene with a melancholy strain of "Youth's a stuff will not endure." But ultimately she was to be rewarded, and a promise, at least, of this came before the announcement of her marriage in the play's closing moments.

In the scene of the baiting of Malvolio, Maria and Toby leave Feste to conclude the mockery. It is a moment of some regret, and we were given a sense that Sir Toby felt the joke had gone too far. "I would we were well rid of this knavery," he says, and admits that he has so greatly offended his niece that he "cannot pursue with any safety this sport to the upshot." He then says: "Come by and by to my chamber." Again, stage business gave a new significance to the words. Before speaking them, he took a ring from his finger and slipped it on to Maria's. Then, when Elizabeth Spriggs played Maria, he took off her glasses. "She puts them back again, but not before a faint smile of timid happiness, on the verge of tears, passes across her face" (Harold Hobson, *Christian Science Monitor,* 17 April 1971). It was a touching moment, again pointed with a strain of "Youth's a stuff will not endure" from Feste. It must be said, I think, that the wistful treatment of Maria represented a directorial imposition. Here, rather than sounding all the notes of the play, John Barton was reducing the spectrum, concentrating on a Chekhovian wistfulness that was not textually justified. It was admirably executed and touching in its effect, but it deprived the play of some of its brighter colors.

The degree of seriousness that should be attributed to the gulling of Malvolio is, I have suggested, an interpretative problem. In spite of the general seriousness of his production, John Barton did not seem to me to be concerned to draw pathos for Malvolio. Both actors who played the role emphasized the grotesque and ludicrous elements in the character enough for us to remain at a distance from him — and after all, his very name suggests that Shakespeare did not think too well of him. There must always be regret that he cannot see the truth about himself, but this fact should also remain prominently before us if the play's ethical structure is to be preserved. Just as Hamlet is given an explanation of why he feels no guilt for the fates of Rosencrantz and Guildenstern, so, I believe, Shakespeare builds in to the last scene of *Twelfth Night* a kind of moral pointer to our attitude towards the way Malvolio has been treated. It is carefully placed just before his final exit. Fabian confesses that he and Sir Toby were responsible for the "device" against Malvolio, but adds:

> How with a sportful malice it was followed,
> May rather pluck on laughter than revenge,
> If that the injuries be justly weighed
> That have on both sides passed. (V.i. 365-8)

These lines were emphasized by Fabian's kneeling to Olivia as he spoke them. Feste, too, reminds us of Malvolio's insults to him in their first scene together, and it is this that provokes Malvolio's exit line: "I'll be revenged on the whole pack of you." As he spoke this, Malvolio removed his chain of office and thrust it into Olivia's hands. The moment was not caricatured. B. A. Young wrote that "the gesture with which he resigns his stewardship, tearing the badge of office from his neck and dropping it in his mistress' hands, is made with such consciousness of rectitude that when he grinds out his departing threat to 'be revenged on the whole pack of you,' we are almost on his side" (*Financial Times,* 22 August 1969). But the other characters had drawn enough of our sympathy to keep the balance in their favor.

A definite decision had obviously been made not to caricature Orsino. He was very well played successively by two actors, both of them fine verse speakers able to suggest in him a luxuriant romanticism that may have been self-indulgent but was not affected. We should, it seems to me, look on Orsino with a kind of indulgent avuncularity. We may shake our heads over his self-absorption, but we should say, with Polonius: "He's far gone; and truly in my youth I suffered much extremity for love, very near this." His love-melancholy was deeply impressed on us even before the performance began. When the first members of the audience were assembling, a lutenist came on to the stage and began to play. Some minutes later, Orsino arrived, tousled, looking as if he suffered from lack of sleep, but sumptuously gowned and richly bejewelled. He threw himself into a chair in a handsomely romantic posture, which he sustained while the lutenist sang him a song by Dowland, "Woeful heart with grief oppressed." As the time for the performance to open approached, Curio entered and the house lights were dimmed; an attendant entered to Curio, who at the end of the song offered some documents to Orsino; he opened them and reflected, but seemed indifferent to their contents. Sounds of the sea were heard as he spoke of music as "the food of love." When his messenger, Valentine, entered, Orsino moved eagerly to meet him and put his hands on his shoulders as he asked for "news of her"; told that Valentine had not been admitted, he sat, "dashed." At the end of the scene he was again offered a paper, but ignored it. The director was creating an image of a noble household whose head bore serious responsibilities but was distracted by passion. Those who served him might deplore it, might worry about its effect on his health; but it was their place to serve him whatever follies he might commit, and this they would not fail to do.

One character in the play has a licence to point out folly wherever he sees it, if only by implication. Already Feste has proved his mistress a fool for being excessively absorbed in romantic nostalgia. When he comes to Orsino's house, he has no direct criticism to offer, but his song, "Come away, death," expresses an exaggeratedly romantic view of love, and has often been interpreted as an oblique criticism of Orsino. Certainly the actor attempted to suggest this view, by singing the second verse as a caricature. The critic of *Punch,* for example, described how Feste circled Orsino "with a curious dragging walk, pressing his hand to his brow, excessively underlining the melancholy until one realizes that the grief expressed *is* excessive. He is using the song as a reproof. Orsino, of course, is too wrapped up in self-pity to notice but Judi Dench's Viola is sharp enough to see what he's on about"

(3 Sept. 1969). Richard David thought this "extraordinary antic mockery" was "a stroke of genius." I was not so sure; it seemed to me rather strained, and I found that spectators who did not know the suggestion that the song has satirical undertones were bewildered by it.

This scene forms the romantic heart of the play. The comedy of Viola's disguise must not for a moment be allowed to obscure this; nor did it. A counterpoint of sea sounds and the lute music for which Orsino calls intensified the emotion of his conversation with Cesario about love, and underlined the fierce passion with which he described his own love as "all as hungry as the sea." Viola's intelligent and sympathetic response to the Duke was an important element in the portrayal of the developing relationship between them. Seated slightly above and behind him, she could convey by her looks something of her tenderness towards him without his noticing it. Richard Pasco, gaunt and hollow-eyed, conveyed a sense of an unexplained passion; it was easy to believe that Orsino's wooing of Olivia became increasingly a frenzied substitute for his repressed feeling for Cesario; the relief when he discovered that Cesario was a girl indeed was the greater for this. Referring particularly to Richard Pasco's handling of Orsino's treatment of Viola in the last scene before discovering her identity, David Isaacs perceptively described the character as "an emotional masochist whose 'You uncivil lady' and 'O, thou dissembling cub' are rapier-like thrusts which may scratch others but which are simultaneously deeper, self-inflicted wounds" (*Coventry Evening Telegraph,* 9 April 1971).

Olivia is a kind of still centre to the play. Wooed by Orsino (via Cesario), Malvolio, Sir Andrew, and Sebastian, she is herself comparatively inactive. Lisa Harrow, a young and beautiful actress, played her as a gentle girl, untutored in the ways of the world, bewildered by the new emotions with which she is assailed but with enough sense of humor to cope adequately with them. The older men around her — Feste, even, initially, Malvolio — were protective towards her, as to a head of a household who commanded their respect even if she had not yet acquired all the authority that the position demanded. She had a warm smile that could express the joy and wonder of her match with Sebastian.

The most important structural element in the play is the long-thwarted relationship between Viola and Sebastian. Their separation has created the tension on which the plot depends; their reunion, expected but delayed, will resolve the complications of the action and bring it to an end. The actor playing Sebastian resembled Judi Dench closely enough for us to feel no embarrassment at the idea that they were twins. He had been likably played, and his relationship with Antonio had been sensibly and sincerely presented. This is crucial to the play's emotional harmony. Antonio is an entirely serious character. He places himself in great danger for Sebastian's sake. Some directors overplay the comedy in his encounter with Cesario, whom he mistakes for Sebastian, but surely in this episode of mistaken identity the emphasis should be on the genuine suffering that Cesario's innocent rejection of him creates. Antonio speaks of Sebastian in idealized terms, as a god to whom he did devotion, who seems now to be vile. The terms of generalized disillusionment that he uses of Sebastian's apparent treachery resemble those of Claudio in his accusation of Hero, and are as deeply felt.

I have described how in the scene with Orsino, Judi Dench reminded us of her dead brother without actually mentioning him. When Antonio accuses her of ingratitude, it is important, of course, that he addresses her as Sebastian. Shakespeare carefully delays this till the climax of his passion, just before the officers accuse him of madness and take him away. Viola has no opportunity to question him, but Judi Dench, cast into rapt wonder, most beautifully conveyed the surge of renewed hope for her brother's safety that this releases in her, culminating in the words quoted in Mrs. Barton's program note: "O, if it prove, / Tempests are kind, and salt waves fresh in love!" This was another point at which modulations of light and sound expanded the stage image, relating this moment of faith and hope to the workings of an eternal providence.

Naturally, these effects were repeated in the last scene when Orsino looks from Sebastian to Viola with the words: "One face, one voice, one habit, and two persons . . ." It is a climactic moment, and Antonio has his place in it. His distress has been reiterated earlier in the scene, during which Shakespeare has gradually brought all the leading characters on the stage and expounded the sufferings of which the cause is, directly or indirectly, the separation of Viola and Sebastian. Antonio suffers because he is denied by Sebastian; Olivia, because she believes that her husband (Sebastian in fact, though she still calls him Cesario) denies her; Orsino, because he believes that the "boy" whom he has loved has deceived him by marrying Olivia. There is thus a solid ground-bass of serious emotion to add weight to the personal joy of the reunions. Viola is unnoticed by Sebastian till after he has addressed Olivia and expressed loving satisfaction at his reunion with Antonio. Only then does he turn to Viola.

The silent moment of confrontation and recognition of the twin brother and sister is the climax of the play. This relationship is the one on which all the others depend. It has seemed impossible of revival, but the impossible has happened; we are in the presence of a miracle. The moment of happiness in Viola and Sebastian spreads to other characters on the stage, creating an emotional solvent in which their problems are resolved; and it spreads to the audience, too. Its theatrical success depends not on any kind of invention or trickery, but on subtle factors of timing and the placing of characters in relation to one another. Traditionally the twins are placed far downstage — that is, close to the audience — for their recognition. The director helped his actors in every possible way. Sound effects, and a hint of sea-mist, recalled Viola's first entry. Lighting concentrated on Viola and Sebastian. Richard David in *Shakespeare Survey* referred to "the sudden freeze of motion and sound as lost sister confronts lost brother with all the other characters forgotten save the enigmatic Feste framed in the background between them" (*Shakespeare Survey 25,* p. 167). After this moment, responsibility shifts from the director to his actors, and they movingly performed their long duologue; Sebastian stepped forward a pace when he first used Viola's name — "Thrice-welcome, drownèd Viola!" — and on Viola's statement of her own identity they embraced. The words here are equivocal. Viola asks her brother not to embrace her till she can produce tangible proofs of her identity, but few directors and actors can resist the temptation to disobey the implicit stage direction; and it may well be that this is right.

After their coming together, attention spread out to those who had been silently watching them. Sebastian hugged both Viola and Olivia when he said to Olivia: "You are betrothed both to a maid and man." When Orsino addressed Viola as "Boy," both Sebastian and Viola turned to him. Viola indicated nervousness; comedy was, quite properly, flowing back into the play, and Feste took charge again, coming forward laughing as the subject of Malvolio was reintroduced. Later in the scene Orsino knelt as he offered his hand in marriage to Viola, and their happiness, along with that of Sebastian and Olivia, was strongly pointed. This was very much in line with Mrs. Barton's observation that at the end of the play the characters divide into two strongly differentiated groups. The lovers "remain privileged inhabitants of Illyria." They made their exit, symbolically, through the back of the tunnel. The others had all departed at one side or other of the stage. Peter Hall had sought a similar effect in his production, in which the lovers could be seen dancing in stately fashion behind a gauze as Feste sang his final song. But here Feste had the stage to himself.

I have referred to Feste from time to time in speaking of other characters. Though he is ubiquitous, he is the only major figure in the play who seems to be content with his own company. He seeks no relationship of affection, except perhaps with the audience, for he stands largely outside the plot, commenting on the characters rather than involving himself with them. He is the hired entertainer, conscious of the need to earn his living, and in his final song he reminds us that all the actors of the play stand in the same relationship to us as he does to them. They, like him, have to "strive to please," in this case for 202 performances. He stands in antithesis to Malvolio who has nothing but enmity for him. Emrys James suggested a quiet wisdom in Feste, and a compassion. One reviewer found him sentimental: "At the end of his performance as Sir Topas, Feste takes off his beard with a weary disgust, and so permits the audience to be completely charmed by him once more . . . Mr. Barton's Feste agrees in a tone of self-redeeming compassion to bring 'the light and paper, and ink' for Malvolio's letter, and so helps us to forget that Shakespeare's fool subsequently and callously fails to deliver the letter itself" (Simon Gray, *New Statesman,* 28 August 1969). Perhaps Emrys James's performance did participate in the emotional, indulgent attitude that John Barton took towards most of the characters of the play; but Feste sees further than Malvolio. Though the wise fool joins in the plot against the foolish wit, there are hints that he acts with the hope of causing Malvolio to see the truth about himself — of making him "the better for his foes" by telling him that he is "an ass" and so causing him to "profit in the knowledge" of himself (V.i. 12-19).

Emrys James and Judi Dench had brought beautiful understanding to their earlier scene together, delicately suggesting a sympathetic respect for one another's independence. It was hinted that he was the only person in the play to see through her disguise. When he says, "Who you are and what you would are out of my welkin," the prompt book records his crossing to her "as if [he] realised who [she] is." The song with which he ends the play was acted out with elaborate mime; he lolled in the fourth stanza, for instance, to imitate the tosspots with drunken heads. He stood for the last verse and left by the side of the stage as the lights faded. He, too, belonged to the world of reality, not of illusion.

When I think in retrospect of this production, it is its beauty that I remember. Not especially — though partly — a visual beauty, but a beauty of communication, of sympathy, understanding, and compassion. It had a Chekhovian quality; and I know that John Barton would regard that as a compliment. It represented a partial reshaping of the play, in its treatment of Maria, at least. But it was honest in its presentation of Malvolio, not sentimentalizing him while allowing him full expression of his limited point of view. Shot through with sadness though the production was, its ultimate effect was a happy one. The sincerity and warmth of the lovers, the happiness of their reunion and the removal of misunderstanding, outweighed the bitterness of Sir Toby and Malvolio. The charm of Lisa Harrow's Olivia, the brilliance of Donald Sinden's comic timing, and above all the exquisitely poetic yet comic Viola of Judi Dench, will remain among my happiest memories of the Stratford theatre.

FOOTNOTES

1. *The Dramatic Essays of Charles Lamb*, edited by Brander Matthews (London, 1891), p. 52.

2. *The Wars of the Roses*, adapted by John Barton (London, 1970), Introduction, p. xxv.

3. In *Shakespearian Comedy*, Stratford-upon-Avon Studies 14, edited by M. Bradbury and D. J. Palmer (London, 1972), pp. 160-180.

IV

John Barton's *Richard II*, 1973-74

Richard Pasco as Richard II and Ian Richardson as Bolingbroke. Photograph by Thomas F. Holte.

John Barton's production of *Richard II* has already received a good deal of academic attention. The designer, Timothy O'Brien, published an article about his designs in *Shakespeare Jahrbuch* in 1975.[1] A student of mine, Mr. J. E. Stredder, wrote an M.A. thesis on the production,[2] and an article by him based on his thesis will appear in the *Shakespeare Jahrbuch* for 1976. Dr. James Tulip, of the University of Sydney, has also published an essay partly concerned with the production.[3] I am, of course, anxious not to duplicate their work, and especially not to appear simply to be cribbing from my own student's thesis. So I feel that I should vary my approach in this lecture, and that I might most usefully talk about the play in terms of the production rather than present a descriptive account of the performance.

The amount of academic attention that this production has already received reflects some of its characteristics. It was in some respects the most strongly interpretative production of a Shakespeare play that I have ever seen. It was also exceptionally stylized. Its most strikingly unusual feature was that two actors, Richard Pasco and Ian Richardson, played the roles of Richard and Bolingbroke alternately. They are perhaps the best equipped classical actors of their generation. Both of them are splendid verse-speakers, experienced actors with grace of movement, expressive gestures, and great capacity to sway and hold an audience. They are also interestingly different from one another. Pasco, taller and of bigger build, has the more obviously 'committed' acting style. He is an emotional actor; his large eyes easily command pathos, his rich, vibrant voice, with a wide tonal range, can be both thrilling and moving. Ian Richardson, slighter in build, is more obviously intellectual. He excels in high comedy and sardonic wit, as may be suggested by the fact that one of his best roles was Vindice in *The Revenger's Tragedy*. He can convey a sense of detachment from the role, a haughty aloofness. His voice is less resonant, but his speaking is brilliantly incisive, calculated and completely controlled. He has enormous technical accomplishment and, perhaps, a more natural bent for comedy than for tragedy.

To see each of these actors within a short space of time as both Richard and Bolingbroke in the same production afforded a fascinating opportunity to consider the contribution of the actor's personality to the role he plays. Bolingbroke is often given to a player of the second rank, and it was interesting to see the part played by a leading actor. But the decision to cast these performers in both roles also had interpretative implications. It has often been said that Richard II is an actor, and, as I shall hope to show, the production explored this aspect of the character. There was also a very strong attempt to show close spiritual resemblances between Richard and Bolingbroke, and this, too, may have been helped by the casting.

The production had numerous other unusual features. It was played on a largely bare stage. At its first appearance, in 1973, there was a narrow, escalator-like structure, receding as it rose higher, on each side of the stage. A platform or bridge spanning the two staircases was normally high above the stage but could ascend or descend. Before the performance began, a pyramid of golden steps was set in the centre of the stage. On it was a kind of scarecrow on which hung the King's robe, surmounted by a mask and a crown. It was at the same time both a symbol of the play's concerns and a declaration of the symbolic method by which they were to be presented. When the production was revived in 1974, the staircase and bridge were no longer used. The stage was cleared, and a golden cloak hung high above the stage as a sun symbol. At the end of the scene, which coincided with the interval, the cloak was released and fluttered down to the stage. There were other alterations, too, most of them reducing the number of symbolic staging devices.

Hobby-horses — that is, costumes which made the actors appear to be riding horses — were used from time to time. They were particularly appropriate for the scene of the lists (I. iii), giving an impression of the pageantry associated with formal jousts and tournaments. Like real horses, they had to be carefully handled. The actors occasionally introduced humanizing touches of comedy by making the horses appear to be restive, and patting their heads to quieten them. I mentioned the platform or bridge which, when the production was first given, spanned the two staircases, and which could ascend and descend. On it Richard could rise and fall, so that, in these performances, "Down, down I come, like glistering Phaëthon," referred to a mechanical rather than a human descent. Richard wore a splendid coat of pleated gold in which, as he spread his arms, he made of himself a visual image of the sun. (In 1974 Richard's descent was down the steps of the central dais.)

The director originally intended that all the characters in the play except the king should wear masks. Timothy O'Brien writes that the idea was to create a sense of the king's isolation, but that it "ran so counter to all that the actors had been taught about the expressive face being the focus of their performances, and so perturbed Bolingbroke, that masks in the end were only used at moments of portent" (p. 117). Even though the consistent use of masks was abandoned, Mr. O'Brien writes that "their depersonalizing influence was at rehearsals and contributed to the intended formality of behavior on the stage in the end" (pp. 117-118). This remark points to another special feature of the production. There was a very conscious stylization of acting method; many speeches were delivered directly at the audience rather than as part of a dialogue among the characters on stage. This created occasional problems. For example, at a dramatic moment in the scene of the lists, the Lord Marshal has to say: "The King hath thrown his warder down" (I.iii.118). The actor told me that if he spoke this line while staring straight at the audience, he roused laughter. The information was obviously redundant. Here, a personal reaction was necessary. He had to turn to watch the king's action, then wheel to face the audience to express his surprise, for the line to be plausible.

In these, and other ways, this was, then, a strongly stylized and symbolical production. It imposed strains upon its audiences. They had to respond to unfamiliar production techniques, and to try to see the point of deliberately unnatural methods of performance which might easily have seemed ludicrous and pretentious. My account so far of the director's methods may suggest tricksiness and gimmickry. The production was accused of these faults. Nevertheless, it was highly successful and was given many performances. It created its own audiences, I think. Though certain aspects of it were strange and initially puzzling, its impact was great and repaid a degree of intellectual and imaginative effort in its audiences. It represented a very serious and intelligent effort to find theatrical correlatives to various features of Shakespeare's playwriting techniques in this early play, and it is in these terms that I should like to consider it. Let me first attempt to characterize some of Shakespeare's aims in writing the play.

Though he worked basically from Raphael Holinshed's massive chronicle history of England, he seems also to have read around the subject a good deal; and he selected from and rearranged historical facts with some freedom. The general tendency of his alterations is to universalize his subject: to tell the story of the reign of Richard II in a manner that brings it into touch with general ideas, and that suggests matters of fundamental human significance behind the particular events that the play dramatizes. The play is much concerned with kingship, with the problems that face an ordinary human being who has to adopt the semi-divine role of king, to try to live up to its responsibilities and make proper use of its privileges. This concern was stressed in the program note that Mrs. Barton wrote for her husband's production. It is headed *The King's Two Bodies,* which is the title of an important book by the historian Ernst Kantorowicz,[4] to which Mrs. Barton refers. This book studies the medieval and Elizabethan doctrine that a king has two bodies, or natures, one "flawless, abstract and immortal," the other "fallible, individual and subject to death and time." This dual nature creates great problems for the man who has to bear it. He is, as it were, an imperfect human being in a guise of perfection, a flawed face behind an idealized mask. As Mrs. Barton wrote, "the Richard of the early scenes is often callous, greedy, frivolous, self-indulgent and unjust . . . A private face that should remain hidden not only manifests itself but contradicts the impersonal mask of kingship by which it should be overlaid." It is clear why the mask was an important symbol in this production.

Another major concern of the play is the relationship between the king and his country, and the plight of a country that is weakly governed. In this of course it reflects contemporary concerns. When Shakespeare wrote it, his Virgin Queen was in her 60s with no obvious heir. It was feared that whoever succeeded to the throne might not match up to the demands of the office, and some of Elizabeth's subjects were even moved to question the validity of the hereditary principle. The queen's susceptibility to influence by favorites provoked direct comparison with Richard II. There were strong movements to depose her. It is interesting that the scene of Richard's deposition was omitted from the three editions of the play published while the queen was still alive. The play must have been thought relevant to the political situation, and eventually it was actually used as a weapon in the political campaign. The Earl of Essex's supporters hired Shakespeare's company of actors to present it as a gesture of support and defiance on the eve of Essex's rebellion. Obviously it was felt, in spite of its historical basis, to deal with live issues. It is especially interesting that Shakespeare and his company were not punished for this special performance. This, surely, is a measure of the extent to which Shakespeare had transcended topicality and presented historical events in a manner that could be regarded as poetical and philosophical rather than political and topical. The relationship between the king and his country is an aspect of this, for the land is seen in the play both as the source of Richard's glory, his "large kingdom," and as the "little grave" which eventually will swallow him. Mr. Barton symbolized the land by a chalice of earth placed centrally to the front of the stage. Several characters took up earth from it at significant points. The gardener planted a sprig in it, when he said of the queen:

> Here did she fall a tear. Here in this place
> I'll set a bank of rue, sour herb of grace.
> Rue even for truth here shortly shall be seen
> In the remembrance of a weeping Queen. (III.iv. 104-107)

And Richard placed his hand close to the chalice on his return from Ireland at the words: "Dear earth, I do salute thee with my hand."

Before starting to write *Richard II,* Shakespeare made a decision of fundamental importance. He decided to write this play entirely in verse. It was a decision he had made three times before, always in history plays: two of the three parts of *Henry VI,* and *King John.* He was never to make the same decision again. Partly this must be the result of the rapid evolution of dramatic styles during the 1590s. *Richard II* must have seemed old-fashioned soon after it was written. Perhaps this is why in 1601 — only about six years after its composition — the actors were able to complain that it was "so old and so long out of use as that they should have small or no company at it."[5] Presumably when he wrote it, Shakespeare was more subservient to the requirements of historical-tragical decorum than he was soon to become. These included the convention that high-ranking characters spoke in verse, and low-ranking ones in prose. In this play, even characters and episodes which might, in a different context, have been represented in prose are given the dignity of verse. This implies, obviously, a degree of stylization and artificiality in the language, and one result of this is that a number of the characters are so lacking in individuality that they seem mainly or entirely choric in function. A partial example is provided by the Duchess of Gloucester. She has only one scene (I.ii). There is some personal force behind her statements as she pleads for revenge against her husband's murderers, yet we feel that the main reason for her presence in the play is as a spokesman of the old order and as a mouthpiece for the conveying of necessary background information. Mr. Barton appropriately presented her in stylized fashion. In 1973 she emerged from a trapdoor, holding a skull above her head and crying "Blood!" to John of Gaunt in tones that were electronically echoed. This created a melodramatic impression which exemplified the dangers of stylization, and in 1974 she simply entered from the wings and spoke quietly, though she still carried the skull.

A similar character is the Welsh Captain, in Act Two, Scene Four. He has a purely choric speech about the state of the country:

> The bay trees in our country are all withered,
> And meteors fright the fixèd stars of heaven.
> The pale-faced moon looks bloody on the earth,
> And lean-looked prophets whisper fearful change . . .

In the note on this scene in my New Penguin edition of the play, which was used for this production, I say that the captain "is important rather for his representative quality than for any personal characteristics." It is an obvious enough comment; I quote it because John Barton's handling of the scene represented a translation into theatrical terms of this kind of critical comment. The captain's speech was spoken not by one man but by eight of them; each of the additional seven was given one line. They stood in a row across the stage in a low light and with their backs to the audience. There was an accompaniment of plaintive horn music. Thus all suggestion of individuality was eliminated, and their choric function was made abundantly plain.

The most obviously choric scene of all is that of the gardeners (III.iv).

As gardeners, they have no reality whatever. They are gardeners simply because this is part of the metaphor that Shakespeare also employs in their language. England has already on a number of occasions been compared to a garden, and now the metaphor is fully expanded and developed:

> Our sea-wallèd garden, the whole land,
> Is full of weeds, her fairest flowers choked up,
> Her fruit trees all unpruned, her hedges ruined,
> Her knots disordered, and her wholesome herbs
> Swarming with caterpillars.

As a literary expression of the state of the kingdom, that is eloquent. It would be entirely at home in an Elizabethan narrative poem. But this is a play, not a poem; and these lines of beautifully controlled, measured, blank verse have to be spoken by someone in the guise of a gardener. What usually happens is that actors seek comic effect, dressing and speaking like the gravediggers in *Hamlet* (who, of course, speak prose), and thus draw attention to themselves, or to the characters they are playing, and away from the meaning of the scene. This is obviously wrong; but to play them as exceptionally well-bred and literate gentlemen who just happen to have taken up gardening as a profession has the equally unsatisfactory effect of sacrificing any sense of reality of the speakers as people. When I was editing the play I did some research into the gardeners of great Elizabethan estates, thinking they might perhaps have been roughly the equivalent of modern professors of botany, or directors of Agricultural Research Stations, but I was not too convinced by what I found. So I thought John Barton hit upon a brilliantly ingenious solution in making them monks, intelligent and literate people who might nevertheless be also full-time gardeners. Quiet organ music was heard in the first part of the scene, with the queen and her ladies; the gardeners sang softly as they entered from the back of the stage. Music accompanied the head gardener's final speech as he took a sprig of rue from his sleeve and planted it in the chalice of earth.

The gardeners' scene represents at an extreme level a procedure which can be observed throughout this play, and which is very much bound up with Shakespeare's decision to write entirely in verse, and in verse of a predominantly plangent, lyrical, elegiac kind that seems almost to have been created for this play. Constantly action as well as language is stylized. Shakespeare seems to be taking the representation of people and events, as of speech, as far away from a naturalistic mode as he dares, rigorously subordinating credibility of immediate effect to the patterns of thought and image that carry the play's truest meanings. Consider for example the way that characters in some of his other plays react to the news that they have been banished. Here is Romeo:

> Ha, banishment! Be merciful, say 'death';
> For exile hath more terror in his look,
> Much more than death. Do not say 'banishment'. (III.ii. 12-14)

Here is Kent in *King Lear:*

> Fare thee well, King. Sith thus thou wilt appear,
> Freedom lives hence, and banishment is here. (I.i. 180-181)

You will remember Coriolanus:

> You common cry of curs, whose breath I hate
> As reek o' th' rotten fens, whose loves I prize
> As the dead carcasses of unburied men
> That do corrupt my air. I banish you. (III.iii. 121-125)

And now here is Mowbray, in *Richard II:*

> A heavy sentence, my most sovereign liege,
> And all unlooked for from your highness' mouth.
> A dearer merit, not so deep a maim
> As to be cast forth in the common air
> Have I deservèd at your highness' hands.
> The language I have learnt these forty years,
> My native English, now I must forgo,
> And now my tongue's use is to me no more
> Than an unstringèd viol or a harp,
> Or like a cunning instrument cased up —
> Or being open, put into his hands
> That knows no touch to tune the harmony. (I.iii. 154-165)

Romeo's reaction is directly related to his feelings for Juliet. He would rather die than be away from her. Kent's is an idiosyncratic expression of his blunt nature and his capacity to make the best of a bad job. Coriolanus's is a wonderfully vivid expression of personal hatred and defiance. But Mowbray's is a meditation on the idea that in a foreign country his language will be of no use to him — not an entirely implausible reaction, but far more important as one in a sequence of passages concerned with the function and power of words, especially a sovereign's words, than as a personal reaction from Mowbray himself. Similarly only a little later, when Bolingbroke and his father, John of Gaunt, discuss the sentence that has been passed, their conversation soon becomes a philosophical discussion on the power of the imagination which is deeply relevant to one of the play's over-riding concerns — for the king rules largely by his power over people's imaginations — but far from a naturalistic representation of a talk between an old father and his newly-banished son.

Such stress in the play's language on the symbolic aspects of the situations portrayed is paralleled by similarly calculated stylization of action. Take for instance Act Three, Scene Two, in which Richard has just returned from Ireland. He speaks his most confident affirmation of the power of kingship:

> Not all the water in the rough rude sea
> Can wash the balm off from an anointed king.
> The breath of worldly men cannot depose
> The deputy elected by the Lord.
> For every man that Bolingbroke hath pressed
> To lift shrewd steel against our golden crown,
> God for his Richard hath in heavenly pay
> A glorious angel. Then if angels fight,
> Weak men must fall; for heaven still guards the right.

Salisbury enters and reports that the Welsh army has defected to Bolingbroke. Richard consoles himself with the thought, "Is not the King's name twenty thousand names?" Immediately Scroop enters and reports Bolingbroke's success in raising troops in England. Richard calls for Bushy, Bagot, and Green and learns that they are dead. And Richard speaks his great meditation on the mortality of kings. The action here is, of course, unhistorical. Shakespeare has compressed events that happened over a period of time at two different places, Barkloughly and Conway. But the reality of the situation is not what matters. There is just enough truth in the happenings to form a structure for Shakespeare's poetic exploration of the polarities of Richard's confidence and despair.

Mr. Barton found several ways of reflecting Shakespeare's dramatic technique in the staging. Richard entered on horseback: not a hobby-horse this time, but a large representation of Roan Barbary, a mythical horse with a unicorn's horn, propelled on skis. Richard looked splendid, with a great plume of feathers above his regal helmet. He dismounted to salute his land. He was all confidence in the opening of the scene, and took a cross from the Bishop of Carlisle as he said:

> For every man that Bolingbroke hath pressed
> To lift shrewd steel against our golden crown,
> God for his Richard hath in heavenly pay
> A glorious angel.

But he let it fall back into Carlisle's hands as he heard of the defection of the Welsh army. After Aumerle's words of encouragement, he remounted the horse. But learning of the deaths of his friends, he let his sword clatter to the ground and himself dismounted, speaking his great lament in a spotlight to the front of the stage. Minor characters spoke most of their lines straight out to the audience, and were symmetrically grouped. Richard left the stage quietly and on foot. The patterning of the action was reflected in the varying symmetries of the stage-picture.

The dramatic method illustrated in this scene, and generally characteristic of the play, throws an emphasis on ideas and their poetical expression rather than on credibility of action and psychologically plausible portrayal of individual personalities. Even characters with quite lengthy roles in this play are formed on similar bases. I have already referred to the Duchess of Gloucester, who has only one scene, which is in effect part of the play's exposition. Richard's queen has an important part to play, but it is not because of anything strongly individual in her personality; indeed, at times she seems almost like an emblematic embodiment of grief. John of Gaunt makes an impact because of his best-known speech, on England — "This royal throne of kings; this seat of Mars" — one of those speeches where the actor's main problem lies in making sure that the audience does not sing along with him. Tony Church delivered it directly to the audience, as a public rather than a private utterance, appropriately since Gaunt is primarily a mouthpiece for certain ideals of kingship and national pride.

These characteristics of the play help to explain and justify the method that John Barton adopted of portraying many of the play's characters. His actors nobly quelled the natural temptation to humanize and round out the outlines of a part. They acted as elements in a somewhat abstract design, not as if each of them was the centre of the design. Sometimes, indeed, Mr. Barton manipulated the play in ways that created an even greater degree of symbolism in character portrayal. The most striking example was the presentation of the Earl of Northumberland's relationship with Bolingbroke. Northumberland was made to seem the active agent in Bolingbroke's rise to the throne. He was unrealistically presented. Towards the end of Act Two, Scene One, he appeared, along with Ross and Willoughby, in a long black robe concealing buskins, high boots which increased his height. In Act Two, Scene Three he rode a big black horse. His power over Bolingbroke was shown to be gradually increasing; correspondingly, Bolingbroke's responsibility seemed less. Northumberland was in charge of the off-stage executions of Bushy and Bagot, and wore black plumes in his helmet. In the episode of Richard's parting from his queen, Northumberland appeared at his most unreal, seeming now a ruthless embodiment of menace and totalitarian power. We heard that he had been spoken of in rehearsals as a "Himmler-figure," a characteristic attempt both to generalize and to find a modern equivalent. The individual was lost in his costume resembling a bird of prey, and towered ominously over the dejected king and queen.

Richard was now "down" indeed. The stylization of costuming extended to the faceless figures on each side of him, riding black hobby-horses, each with a rope attached to one of Richard's arms.

You will perhaps have noticed that there are two distinct processes in the production methods that I have been describing. One is an effort to devise methods that will find appropriate theatrical conventions to mirror the particular dramatic conventions of this play. The other is one that may be said to build still further upon these theatrical conventions. In his presentation of the relationship between Northumberland and Bolingbroke, the director was creating a simplified pattern from Shakespeare's multiplicity of suggestiveness. Partly he was reinforcing structural patterns that are present in Shakespeare's text; partly he was distorting them. These processes were observable elsewhere. At times they resulted in clear improvements. The scene of the gages, for example, has often caused embarrassment in the theatre. Bagot accuses Aumerle of responsibility for Gloucester's death. Aumerle rejects the accusation, throwing down his glove as a challenge. Fitzwater repeats the accusation and throws down his glove. Percy does the same; so does another, anonymous Lord. The Duke of Surrey throws *his* glove down, taking Aumerle's part. Finally Aumerle borrows another glove and throws *that* down as another challenge. The highly patterned action is obviously calculated, but, as gloves gradually pile up on the stage, it is in danger of seeming ludicrous. In performance this scene has usually been shortened or omitted. If you had smuggled a text into the Royal Shakespeare Theatre, you would have found that though the episode was included, Mr. Barton had so rearranged the lines and reassigned the speeches that he had virtually rewritten the scene. It came over powerfully, with no hint of comedy.

Other scenes that have often been omitted are those concerned with Aumerle's conspiracy and his mother's attempts to save him from its consequences. The scenes are technically somewhat immature. Shakespeare is trying, not quite successfully, to achieve a subtle fusion of seriousness and comedy for which he cannot command the necessary technical resources, so that the comedy tends to submerge the seriousness. But there are good reasons for including the scenes, and the awkwardnesses in the writing can be mitigated by tactful acting. Sir John Gielgud wrote in an introduction to the play: "The character of York . . . can be of great value, provided that the actor and director can contrive between them a tactful compromise between comedy and dramatic effect."[6] John Barton had good actors in the roles, and he wisely permitted here a more naturalistic, personal style of acting. By relaxing the stylization evident elsewhere, he was facing up to the problems of the episode and making the best of it, rather than evading the issue by the drastic cutting to which many directors have resorted in desperation of making the scenes work.

Although, as I have insisted, many of the lesser characters in this play are important rather as elements in a design than as individual human beings, nevertheless, at the center of the design is one supremely important figure, and another who is scarcely less so. Richard and Bolingbroke are rather like the figures on a weather clock. As one goes in, the other comes out; and, it would seem, with almost as little exercise of their own will-power. This see-saw element in the play became the mainspring of the production, though not without textual manipulation and distortion, to some of which I have already referred. In her program note, Mrs. Barton wrote: "Like the two buckets filling one another that Richard imagines in the deposition scene, buckets which take a contrary course within the deep well of the crown, Richard's journey from king to man is balanced by Bolingbroke's progress from a single to a twin-natured being. Both movements involve a gain and a loss. Each, in its own way, is tragic."

As a generalized critical statement, that is acceptable. But as such it is inevitably a simplification. There are implications of tragedy in the portrayal of Bolingbroke, especially if we read his part in this play in the light of the extended portrait of him given in Parts One and Two of *Henry IV;* but I should find it difficult to argue, and I do not suppose that Mrs. Barton would argue, that the Bolingbroke of *Richard II* is a fully realized tragic figure. The suggestion of equivalence between Richard and Bolingbroke which Mr. Barton's production undoubtedly gave required the importation of lines from *2 Henry IV* and the transference of an important passage in *Richard II* to Bolingbroke from another character. Latent in the casting, it was made in the production even before the first words were spoken; and it was linked with an image to which I have already referred. Mrs. Barton pointed to Shakespeare's exploration of "the latent parallel between the King and that other twin-natured human being, the Actor. Like kings, actors are accustomed to perform before an audience. Like kings, they are required to submerge their own individuality within a role and, for both, the incarnation is temporary and perilous. Like the two kings in *Richard II,* their feelings towards their roles are often ambiguous, a mixture of exhilaration and disgust. And . . . Richard is intensely conscious, in the early scenes, of kingship as a role to be acted." An introductory mime impressed this parallel upon us.

Before the house lights dimmed there appeared a figure resembling Shakespeare, carrying a book resembling the First Folio, printed seven years after he died. He contemplated the robed scarecrow, opened the book, and signalled for the appearance of the actors. They filed on in two columns, one headed by Ian Richardson, the other by Richard Pasco. They all wore rehearsal costume. The leaders of the company joined Shakespeare at the dais, each holding one side of the book. Shakespeare mounted the pyramid, took from the scarecrow the crown and the mask, and placed them on the open book. The two actors held the crown and mask high between them; Shakespeare bowed to the actor who was to play Richard at that performance, and gradually the actors took on their costumes and wigs, in view of the audience, assuming the appearance of the characters they were to play. The robing of Richard was a kind of coronation ritual; the court knelt to him, chanting words not in the text: "God save the King! Long live the King! May the King live forever!" Richard faced the audience, echoed "May the King live forever!" and removed his mask.

Thus the director prefigured the play's concern with the inevitable tension between the demands made by the office of kingship, of being God's deputy on earth, and the capacities of the human being who has to try to fill a role that is inevitably too big for him. And, even more important to this production, he associated this with the idea of the actor assuming the role that he had to play on stage. The human being who has to play the king in real life was paralleled with the actor who has to play the role of king in the theatre.

Although *Richard II* is more thoroughly poetic and verbalized than some of Shakespeare's later plays, it still leaves quite a lot to the actors. Richard does not say very much in the earlier part of the play; Bolingbroke does not say much in the later. The actors must decide how to interpret their silences. Richard, in his first scene, is visually dominant but says little. Should the actor attempt thus early to suggest anything positive about Richard's personality, or should he hold back? In the past, actors have added business here to create a more positive impact. Beerbohm Tree and F. R. Benson are famous for having had Richard caress and feed hounds in bored indifference; later in the play, one of the hounds was seen to have transferred allegiance to Bolingbroke. Gielgud suggests that the actor "must use the early scenes to create an impression of slyness, petty vanity, and callous indifference." Yet the quarrel between Bolingbroke and Mowbray is about a matter in which the King is deeply implicated — the murder of the Duke of Gloucester. Both of Mr. Barton's actors, quite rightly, showed Richard's silence as the reverse of indifference, rather a careful keeping silent in the knowledge that Richard might at any moment be directly accused.

Richard's behavior in the first part of the play becomes progressively worse, culminating in his brutal treatment of John of Gaunt, whose speech about what England ought to be serves as a measure of Richard's personal disqualifications for the kingly office. But it would not be disputed, I think, that after his return from Ireland, as the tide of fortune turns against him,

Shakespeare gradually reinstates him in the audience's favor. An interpretative problem arises over the presentation of Richard's relations with his
favorites, Bushy and Green. In Act Three, Scene One, Bolingbroke accuses
them of having

> Made a divorce betwixt his [Richard's] Queen and him,
> Broke the possession of a royal bed.

Some critics and actors have interpreted this as an accusation against
Richard of homosexuality. This belief can color an actor's entire interpretation of the role. But the portrayal of Richard's relationship with his queen
in the rest of the play does nothing to support the accusation. I do not think
we can say precisely what Shakespeare had in mind; but in Mr. Barton's
production, the suggestion was not merely avoided but actively negated.
When the Duke of York heard the accusation he reacted with incredulity, in
a way that suggested it reflected discredit on whoever made it rather than
on Richard, against whom it is made. Even before his return from Ireland,
then, Richard was rising in the audience's sympathy.

One important symbol in this production was a mirror. Shakespeare
himself calls for it, but Mr. Barton made much more extensive use of it than
the text requires. The actors as actors used a mirror in the introductory
mime, as they put on their costumes. Richard used the mirror more than once
in the scene of the lists; indeed, he decided to go to Ireland only when he
realized "how splendid he will look in armour (he holds his plumed helmet in
the crook of his arm and reviews himself in the mirror)" (Stredder, p. 51).
The mirror was thus established as a symbol of Richard's vanity before he
called for it in the deposition scene (IV.i). In describing some of the techniques of the production, I have said little of the acting, but I should like to
pay tribute, particularly, to Richard Pasco's treatment of this passage. We
had a powerful sense of impotent and frustrated rage as he dashed his hand
through the glass. Peter Thomson described the sequel[7] with a perceptive
sense of its symbolism: "When Richard had punched out the glass,
Bolingbroke lifted the empty ring-frame and placed it over Richard's head
deliberately enough for us to see it pass from halo to crown, and from crown
to noose to the enormously stressed accompaniment of

> The shadow of your sorrow hath destroy'd
> The shadow of your face. (IV. i. 292-3)"

These lines were repeated, chanted in chorus, by the attendant lords. There
was self-pity in Richard's action, perhaps, but there was strength, too; the
strength of a man who, though he had been stripped of both the fantasies and
the realities of monarchy — he now wore a simple gown — still had the
strength to seek to know the truth about himself. For me, this was the

emotional climax of the performance. Richard wore the empty frame of the mirror round his neck in the scene with his queen on the way to the Tower and it was still there for the opening of his soliloquy shortly before his death in Pomfret Castle.

Whereas the growth of sympathy for Richard grows naturally from the text of the play, Bolingbroke's position in this respect is more problematical. The mere fact that he takes the place of the deposed King may turn us against his sinister, largely silent presence. "As he assumes the King's role," Mrs Barton wrote, he "becomes silent, impersonal and remote: his thoughts and emotions concealed behind a mask." We are shown little of his inner feelings. Shakespeare gives him no soliloquy.

But in the production, much was different. Mr. Barton clarified, strengthened, and simplified Bolingbroke's role. The idea of becoming king was shown to have occurred to him earlier than in Shakespeare's text. After his banishment, his father, John of Gaunt, bidding him farewell, drew the shape of a crown in the air over his head — quite improperly, I thought considering Gaunt's steadfast allegiance to the old order. In the same episode, the director added to Bolingbroke's final speech the line: "Now must I serve a long apprenticehood." This adapts Bolingbroke's words "Must I not serve a long apprenticehood / To foreign passages" (I. iii. 271-2) but the inescapable implication was that he would be apprenticed to the monarchy. I have described already the symbolical presentation of North umberland as a way of minimizing Bolingbroke's guilt. In the trial of Bushy and Green, Bolingbroke did not speak the charges as from himself, but read them with obvious distaste from a document which Northumberland handed to him. The clear implication was that they were trumped-up charges.

Mr. Barton even gave Bolingbroke the soliloquy that Shakespeare failed to provide. It came at the beginning of Act Five, Scene Three, in which Shakespeare himself shows the new king unhappy at the absence of his son and experiencing some of the trials and tribulations of kingship. Mr. Barton inserted a speech which began with an abbreviated version of the same character's lament on his sleeplessness from 2 Henry IV (III. i. 4-9, 12-14), continued with four-and-a-half lines spoken by Warwick in the same play (III. i. 80-84), four-and-half lines already spoken by Richard in Richard I. (V.i. 55-9), and three-and-a-half lines based on more of Henry's speeches in 2 Henry IV (IV.v. 185, 197-8, III. i. 30-31). The gist of this extraordinary piece of cobbling was a meditation on royal sleeplessness, and awareness on Henry's part that he has been placed where he is by Northumberland and that civil war will ensue. The soliloquy ended with words from 2 Henry IV:

Happy low, lie down!
Uneasy lies the head that wears the [*sic*] crown!

On the last line, a group of lords came out of the shadows behind Henry,
echoing the line, and a bridge passage was concocted from the lines following
this in *2 Henry IV*. In the final scene, too, a skilful series of readjustments of
emphasis drew sympathy for Bolingbroke at Northumberland's expense.
The heads of the executed noblemen were brought in by Northumberland's
men, impaled on pikes, whereas in the text they are merely mentioned.
Richard's disgust at this brutality was clear. Harry Percy's accusation
against the Bishop of Carlisle was reassigned to his father, Northumberland, and Bolingbroke's forgiveness of Carlisle became a calculatedly
rebellious revulsion against Northumberland's domination.

The manipulation of Bolingbroke's role, and the additions to it, were
clearly designed to increase sympathy for him, to suggest in him an awareness of a cyclical element in human history, and to bring him closer to
Richard. This design was completed in the prison scene.

At the end of Richard's soliloquy, a groom enters to him. He has with
some difficulty got permission to come to visit his old master, whom he
saddens with the story of how Richard's horse, Roan Barbary, carried the
usurper, Bolingbroke, to his coronation. This tiny but striking episode has its
place in the design of the play. The common people have few representatives
in *Richard II*. The groom is one of them, and his final allegiance helps to bind
us to Richard in his last moments. He was played as a hooded figure with a
rustic accent. When Richard had said,

I was not made a horse,
And yet I bear a burden like an ass,
Spurred, galled, and tired by jauncing Bolingbroke (V.v. 92-4),

he suddenly recognized the man before him. The groom threw back his hood
and revealed himself as Bolingbroke in disguise. Richard took from his own
neck the frame of the mirror and held it between them, so that each saw the
other as if he were a reflection of himself. The director seemed intent on
suggesting a recognition on Bolingbroke's part that both he and Richard have
been the playthings of fortune, both finally united in a Wilfred Owen-like
"strange meeting" in which their shared experience of the hollowness of the
kingly crown draws them together more powerfully than their former rivalry
sets them apart. Here we saw them as themselves, neither needing to act a
part. They knelt for a moment in this pose before Bolingbroke left on the line:
"What my tongue dares not, that my heart shall say."

It was a theatrically impressive moment, and represented an extension
of something that is genuinely present in the play as Shakespeare wrote it. I

confess all the same that I found it strained. Mr. Barton said during a public discussion at which I took the chair that he intended it as "a subliminal moment, so that though it is meaningful to Richard, he cannot actually tell whether it was dream or reality." And Mr. O'Brien writes: "Was it the King's eyes that gave to the groom the face of Bolingbroke?" (p. 119). This uncertainty might have been conveyable in the cinema by some kind of superimposition of images, but in the theatre we could not help identifying the actor as Bolingbroke. The confrontation seemed to demand an explanation that was not provided by the dialogue, and it conflicted with the line Richard has to say only a few moments later, when he attacks the keeper with the words, "The devil take Henry of Lancaster and thee," a line which surely denies the implication that there is explicit fellow-feeling between the two men. It illustrates a danger of Mr. Barton's production-methods; that, at their extremes, they were directing their audience what to think, instead of stimulating their imaginations to think it.

Here, it seemed to me, the director achieved theatrical effectiveness at the expense of our credulity. It was not a cheap theatricality, because it epitomized one aspect of the director's interpretation of the play; but it labored the point. I had, however, nothing but admiration for a piece of theatrical trickery at the end of the performance. The play had begun with the investiture of an actor as King Richard II. It seemed about to end with the final investiture, following Richard's death, of Bolingbroke as King Henry IV. Exton entered with the coffin of Richard, whom he had brutally murdered. Ian Richardson, when he played Bolingbroke, fell upon the coffin with a great cry of anguish, as if for his dearest friend. Mournful music sounded, and on the play's last line the coffin descended, as if into a vault. Coronation music returned, and the figure of Shakespeare, seen at the beginning of the play, appeared as if to crown Bolingbroke, who turned towards him, his back to the audience. Drums rolled powerfully in crescendo. Courtiers gathered around Bolingbroke. He was invested with the golden robe of kingship. All but two of his courtiers fell away, the music reached a climax, and the king turned to us. The drums suddenly ceased, and the courtiers beside Bolingbroke threw back their hoods and revealed themselves, one as the actor who had been playing Richard, the other as the actor who had been playing Bolingbroke. The robes between them, though glittering, were empty. The face was not that of King Richard, nor of King Henry. It was the face of the eternal king who keeps his court within the "mortal temples of a king." It was the face of death.